youth football coaching

sessions

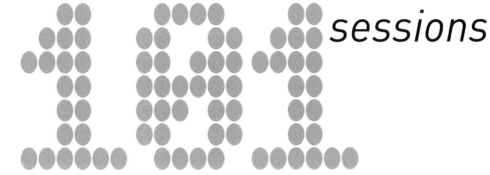

Also available from Bloomsbury in this series

101 Youth Rugby Drills – 2nd edition
Chris and Anna Sheryn

101 Youth Football Drills – 3rd edition
Age 12–16
Malcolm Cook

101 Youth Cricket Drills
Age 7–11
Luke Sellers

101 Youth Fitness Drills
Age 7–11
John Shepherd and Mike Antoniades

tony charles
stuart rook

youth football coaching

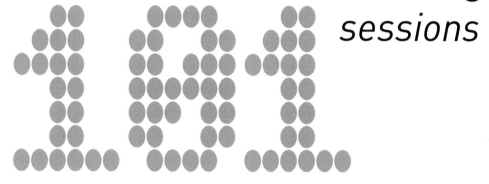

sessions

B L O O M S B U R Y
LONDON · NEW DELHI · NEW YORK · SYDNEY

Published in 2011 by
A & C Black, an imprint of
Bloomsbury Publishing Plc
50 Bedford Square
London WC1B 3DP
www.bloomsbury.com

Reprinted 2013 and 2014

ISBN 978 14081 3079 7

Acknowledgements
Designer James Watson
Cover artwork © Tom Croft, cover image © Shutterstock
Textual illustrations courtesy of Mark Silver
All photographs courtesy of Getty

Note: While every effort has been made to ensure that the content of this book is as technically accurate and as sound as possible, neither then authors nor the publishers can accept responsibility for any injury or loss sustained as a result of the use of this material.

Bloomsbury uses paper with elemental chlorine-free pulp, harvested from managed sustainable forests.

Typeset in 10pt on 12pt Din Regular by Margaret Brain, Wisbech, Cambridgeshire
Printed and bound in Great Britain by CPI Group (UK) Ltd, Croydon CR0 4YY

10 9 8 7

CONTENTS

FOREWORD

Having worked with hundreds of players in my capacity as a coach, choreographer and professional footballer, I totally understand the power of football and the social benefits it provides. I believe that *101 Youth Football Coaching Sessions* by Tony Charles and Stuart Rook has adopted a unique approach to session planning and coaching. This is a book like no other, one that features a broad range of coaching topics which ensures children of all ages can participate in and enjoy football, regardless of their level of ability, as every game is fun and inclusive.

Furthermore, you can combine a number of warm-ups, games and exercises to create an entire session tailored to your coaching requirements. This can be achieved with ease by following the 'session plans' at the back of the book or by simply selecting a combination of sessions yourself.

101 Youth Football Coaching Sessions has successfully brought together the vast experience of community and advanced coaching in an easy to follow and practical session book. This book is an essential resource for any aspiring coach, teacher, youth worker or anyone with an interest in developing grass roots football players.

Andy Ansah
Football Consultant and Choreographer

INTRODUCTION

The main purpose of this book is to help coaches and players to get the most out of their coaching sessions. By combining our three decades of experience we have created 101 fun, informative and challenging coaching sessions, designed to give players the maximum time with the football, to enable them to improve their football skills. We believe that young players learn best when they are enjoying themselves and have accordingly designed this book around this principle by incorporating fun, fast-paced warm ups, free-flowing imaginative technical sessions and challenging small-sided game practices.

We have designed each session to be as inclusive as possible, with as many players working with a ball, or a ball between two or three, as often as it is viable, depending on the technique coached during the exercise. This is in order to move away from old-fashioned line drills, where the players are static and have to wait for their turn and might only touch a football once every few minutes. Giving players more touches of the ball will only help in their overall development. From our experience, when working with children the more involved they are and the more enjoyment the session brings, the less likely they are to be disruptive or become disengaged from the session.

Each page in the book gives you a diagram showing how to set out the session along with sub headings, which help you with the following crucial areas of your session:

- *Organisation* – how to set out the correct sized area and how to organise the players, which players need a ball or a bib and if there is any particular requirement for the setting up of the session.
- *Equipment* – what specific equipment you will need to deliver the session.
- *Description* – a description of the rules of the game and how it should work successfully. This will point out the basic objective of the game and how to find a winner of each game in order to make it competitive.
- *Coaching points* – the key coaching points of the session which you need to try to get across to the players. For each game we have listed three or four coaching points but feel free to include your own.
- *Progressions* – how to make the game more difficult. Some of the games are very basic and can be progressed quite quickly, others are a little bit more difficult to grasp and might take longer for the players to master. One of the most important aspects of being a coach is knowing when the group of players need to be progressed and their skills further challenged.
- *Instructions* – this sub heading appears only in a small number of sessions and relates to specific extra instructions that the coach will need to call out during the course of the practice.

Learning how to plan a session is one of the most important skills a coach can have. Understanding the level of ability, age range and level of development of the players you coach will help you to know what you can coach, what skills you need to coach and how you are going to coach those skills, and is essential in the development of your players. Remember, plan your work and work your plan!

The sessions

With the exception of the warm-ups, at the end of each session you will find a series of numbers – these are session numbers and relate to other games within the book. We have carefully selected games that we feel work well with others to make up a complete football coaching session. Warm-ups can be applied to any session and what we have suggested here is simply a guide for you to work from and develop your own coaching sessions, as we feel a coach should be adaptable and, above all, imaginative.

The complete sessions we have suggested (indicated by the >>> symbol usually consist of two or three fun football sessions and one or two small-sided games. All of these sessions will correspond to the technique being coached during the practice. For example: Session 22 – 'Body ball' is a dribbling game that we've matched with fun football games 28 – 'Shark attack', 32 – 'King of the ring' and 68 – 'Skillz school', which are all dribbling sessions, and small-sided game 78 – 'Four corners', where the idea of the game is to dribble the ball into the corner in order to score a goal. This encourages the players to apply the dribbling techniques that they have learned during the fun games to their play in a conditioned small-sided game.

In each session we have also suggested where the coach should position him or herself to be able to view and correct the technique of players and to deliver the coaching points and progressions effectively, which will help the players to get the most out of the session. It will also ensure that the coach can survey the entire area and see everything that is happening on a wider scale, particularly during the small-sided games. Being able to see the 'bigger picture' is an essential coaching skill and incorporating this into your sessions will help the players develop into more complete footballers.

The position of the coach suggested in each session means the coach will not be interfering with play, allowing it and therefore the session to flow freely, while maintaining control from a broader viewpoint.

The timing for each session will depend on the age group and length of your session. For example, an hour-long after-school club might consist of a warm-up game (5–10 minutes), a fun football game (15–20 minutes), then a conditioned small-sided practice (10–15 minutes), which would then naturally develop into a practice match at the end.

For a 90-minute or two-hour session you might want to spend more time on a specific technique or on two different techniques, incorporating three or four different fun football games – or you may wish to spend more time on the small-sided game conditioned practices. In this instance, a longer warm-up would benefit the players by preparing them for a longer session. The warm-up games can also be used as a cool down at the end of the session.

Club coaches may well be able to identify an area that they feel needs specific improvement in their team, and should design a session plan with that goal in mind. Being able to spot certain strengths and weaknesses in a team or a player and then planning how to improve on those weaknesses or make best use of the strengths could mean the difference between a good team and a great team.

We believe that to be a good coach you need to let your personality come across in your sessions. Each page is a guide for you to use: feel free to adapt any game to allow it to work best for you.

Finally, our biggest hope is that this book will inspire coaches, teachers and parents to develop fresh, entertaining and informative sessions and that they will always be positive, show encouragement and provide examples of fair play. Keep up the good work and keep laying the foundations for the football futures of young players.

Happy coaching!

ABOUT FOUNDATION FOOTBALL

Foundation Football is dedicated to improving the quality of coaching to young players. It is one of London's leading independent, award-winning coaching companies, coaching children from Key Stage 1 upwards. We have coached across Europe, North America and Asia with the aim of improving the quality of coaching to boys and girls of all ages and abilities, hopefully laying the foundations for their football futures.

Foundation Football believes all children, whatever their circumstances or level of ability, should be able to participate in and enjoy sport. It can improve a child's confidence, encourage them to get involved with the session, to have and to learn the skills to participate and to show a desire to improve and achieve.

Foundation Football provides children with the opportunity to access sport during the school day and also evenings, weekends and school holidays. We also provide Local Education Authorities with delivery of sessions, tournaments and competitions.

Our enthusiastic coaches give a level of enthusiasm that will meet the energetic needs of every child, delivering sports coaching sessions in primary and secondary schools through fun and informative sessions with fresh ideas. They are all qualified, are always positive role models, show encouragement and provide examples of fair play.

If you require further information about Foundation Football please visit **www.foundationfootball.com**.

ACKNOWLEDGEMENTS

We would like to thank all of the coaches from Foundation Football for their valuable input, particularly Leon Othen and Peter McGillicuddy.

WARMING UP

Warming up is one of the most important aspects of your coaching session. It is vital that your players are warmed up properly in order to maximise their performance and reduce the risk of injury. A warm-up also helps the players to concentrate on the session ahead.

All these warm-up sessions can be used at the beginning of any coaching session as they are inclusive and not restricted to one specific football technique. Particular emphasis is given to the importance of developing and mastering the basic physical skills of agility, balance, coordination and speed, along with spatial awareness.

A good warm-up is a fundamental part of ensuring a productive coaching session. An active warm-up will prepare your players physically by gently increasing the heart rate, and also ensure players are mentally focused on the session to follow.

session 1   traffic lights

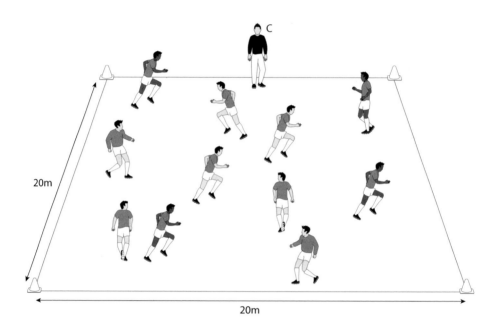

Organisation: Set out a 20 x 20m area.

Equipment: Bibs, marker cones, footballs.

Description: Players move around inside the area listening to the coach's instructions. Each instruction gives a simple movement for players to follow.

Examples of instructions: Green light = go (move around the area); red light = stop (stand still); yellow light = get ready to go (jog on the spot); reverse = move around the area backwards; speed bump = players lie down on their back on the floor (if it's not wet or muddy).

Coaching points: Encourage lots of movement. Spatial awareness – don't crash into another player. Listening skills.

Progressions: Coach makes up more commands (examples). Add a ball per player, now each player dribbles a ball while trying to listen to and perform each command.

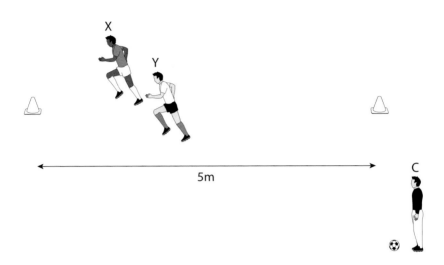

Organisation: Set up two cones 5m apart. Players stand facing each other, in between the two cones. Create sufficient areas for the number of players.

Equipment: Marker cones, one football between two.

Description: One player leads (X), the other copies (Y). The lead has to touch a cone to the left or right before the copier (mirror) gets there by trying to outwit their opponent using a 'fake', dropping the shoulder to move one way then actually moving the other way. Once a cone is touched with the hand that player gets a point and the players switch roles.

Coaching points: Keep low to make it easier to react to your partner's movement. Stay on your feet. Make your 'fake' believable, drop your shoulder and try to change direction more than once.

Progression: Use a 'double fake' to lose your opponent, move both ways to try to lose your defender. Introduce a football, now the ball must touch the cone to win a point. Remember, mirrors can't tackle their opponent, but they can move side to side to block each cone.

session 3 — wake the giant

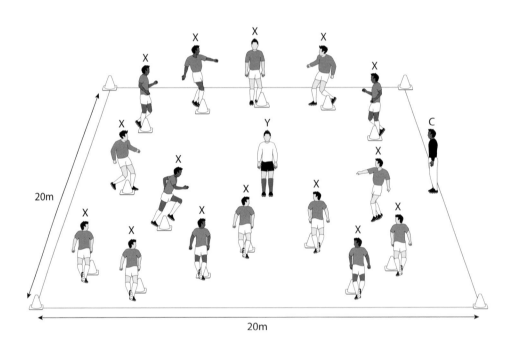

20m

20m

Organisation: Set out a 20 x 20m area. The correct amount of cones are randomly scattered around the area for the amount of players, so that each (X) player can stand behind one cone each. One player (Y) stands in the middle of the area.

Equipment: Marker cones, one bib, footballs.

Description: On the coach's command the X players creep up to Y ('the giant'). Y has his eyes closed and stands so that he cannot see the X players approaching. On the coach's command, Y opens his eyes and tries to 'tag' as many players as possible. If the X players make it to a cone they are 'safe'. Players that are tagged are now out and stand with the coach. The aim for the X players is to sneak up to 'the giant' and tag them on the back before they turn around.

Coaching points: Observation – watch the giant and his/her movements. React quickly to escape from the giant. Once you have a ball keep it close to your feet (during progression).

Progressions: Add an extra giant. Give each player a ball. Dribble the ball using left or right foot only.

session 4   derby day

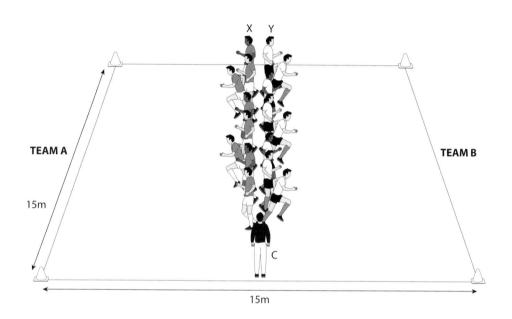

Organisation: Set out a 15 x 15m area. Players are on two teams (X/Y). The coned lines on the left and the right, which mark out the area, are named after two local rival teams, creating a derby atmosphere! The players are separated into two teams and line up in the middle of the area in single file – one behind the other, players alternate each time (see diagram).

Equipment: Bibs, marker cones, footballs.

Description: On the coach's command the players run to the team line called out and return. The first team to return is awarded a point. The coach can try to confuse the players to make it difficult, for example pointing to one line, but calling the command for the other line.

Coaching points: Listening skills. Observation. Encourage lots of movement. Keep the ball close to your feet (during dribbling progression).

Progressions: Introduce a football per player; the players now dribble up to and away from the team line. Once at the team line perform a 'fake'. Use a different turn each time.

session 5 head catch

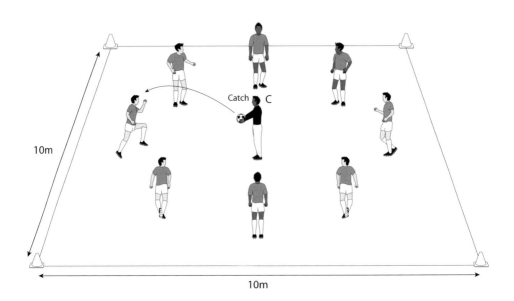

Organisation: In a 10 x 10m area, arrange the players in a circle with the coach standing in the middle.

Equipment: Marker cones, one football.

Description: The coach takes turns moving around the circle to each player and calls either 'head' or 'catch'. The player does the opposite action to that which is called, so for 'head' they catch the ball and for 'catch' the player heads the ball back to the coach. If the player gets the action wrong they are out – last player standing is the winner!

Coaching points: Listening skills. React as quickly as you can. Use your forehead when heading the ball.

Progressions: If the player gets it wrong, they go onto one knee. The coach throws the ball around the circle to players in a random order.

session 6 heads, shoulders, knees and ball

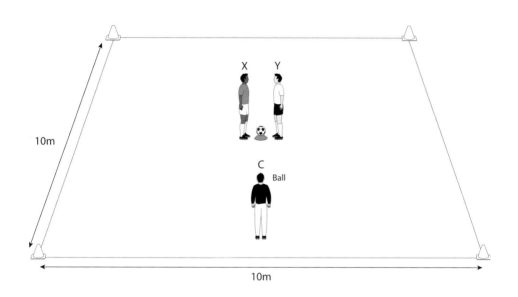

Organisation: Set out a 10 x 10m area. Two players stand opposite each other with a ball balanced on a cone in between them. Create sufficient areas for the number of players.

Equipment: Marker cones, footballs.

Description: As the coach calls out a body part the player has to touch that part of their body. For example, when the coach calls 'head' the player touches their own head. When the coach calls 'ball' the first player to grab the ball is the winner!

Coaching points: Listening skills. React as fast as possible to beat your partner to the ball.

Progressions: Players start with their back to the ball so they have to turn and grab the ball. Play in groups of three.

session 7 protect the king

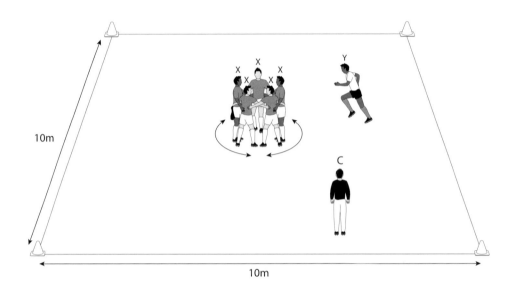

Organisation: Set out a 10 x 10m area. Organise all of the players into a circle, facing inwards with arms linked so they are huddled together (X players). One player is named 'the king' and places a bib into the waistband of their shorts, hanging down like a tail. Another player, (Y) stands separate from the circle of (X) players.

Equipment: Bibs, marker cones, footballs.

Description: Working together, the X players have to protect their 'king' player from having the bib pulled out by the Y player by moving clockwise and anti-clockwise.

Coaching points: Move your circle around quickly. Communication is key. Work as a team to protect your king.

Progressions: Add more X players to make a bigger circle. The Y player dribbles a ball.

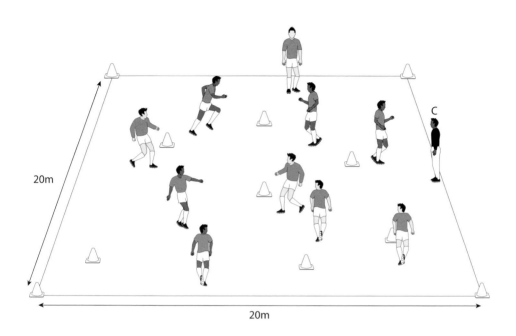

Organisation: Set out a 20 x 20m area. Scatter cones randomly around the area. There should be fewer cones than players.

Equipment: Bibs, marker cones.

Description: Players move around the area. When the coach shouts 'Cones!' the players run and stand by the nearest cone. Any player who doesn't find a cone runs to another player and says 'Excuse me please'. This player then has to move and find a new cone and the second player takes his place. Any player without a cone after a 10 second countdown by the coach is out of the game or performs a fun forfeit.

Coaching points: Encourage movement. Spatial awareness. Use your speed and acceleration to get to each cone quickly.

Progressions: Change movement to skipping, hopping and moving backwards or sideways. Reduce countdown time to 5 seconds. Reduce the number of cones, therefore increasing the number of players who go out or do a forfeit.

session 9 mr ice

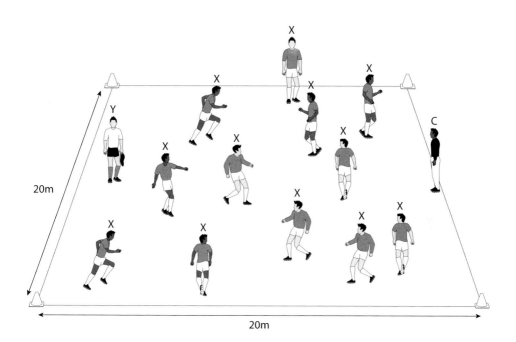

Organisation: Set out a 20 x 20m area.

Equipment: Bibs, marker cones.

Description: Mr Ice (Y) holds a bib in their hand and runs around the area trying to tag the other players (X). Once tagged the players freeze and are out of the game. Ensure that each player is tagged with the bib being held rolled up in a ball in the hand, and not being thrown at other players.

Coaching points: Encourage lots of movement. Spatial awareness. Use body swerves to lose Mr Ice.

Progressions: Add another Mr Ice, or Mrs Ice! Add a Mr Fire, who unfreezes the frozen players, allowing them to rejoin the game.

session 10 ball of life

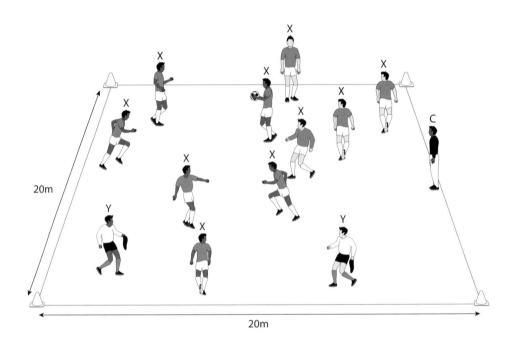

Organisation: Set out a 20 x 20m area.

Equipment: Bibs, marker cones, one football.

Description: Select two taggers (Y players), who each hold a bib. When the coach says 'go' they have to try to tag an X player. If an X player is tagged, they take the bib and become a 'tagger'. However, all of the X players have one ball between them and may pass the ball to each other using their hands. Whenever an X player has the ball in their hands they are safe, and cannot be tagged.

Coaching points: Encourage lots of movement. Spatial awareness. Teamwork, share the 'ball of life' with your teammates to prevent them from being tagged.

Progressions: Add another Y player. Limit the amount of time any player can hold the ball of life to 5 seconds. X players pass the ball with their feet.

session 11 world cup warm-up

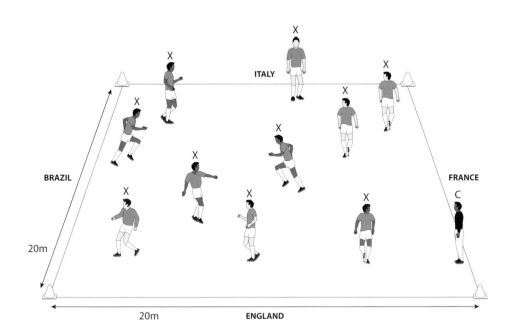

Organisation: Set out a 20 x 20m area and name each side of the area after a famous World Cup-winning team.

Equipment: Bibs, marker cones, footballs.

Description: The players move around inside the area. When the coach calls the name of the country all the players run to that side as fast as possible.

Coaching points: Encourage plenty of movement. Spatial awareness. Keep the ball close to the feet (during dribbling progression).

Progressions: Change movements to forwards/backwards, side-to-side, skips, over the gates. Last player to arrive at the line is out of the game or does a fun forfeit. Give each player a ball, players dribble around area and to each line.

session 12 remote control

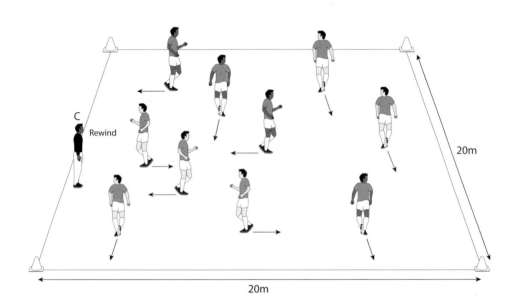

Organisation: Set out a 20 x 20m area.

Equipment: Bibs, marker cones, footballs.

Description: The players move around inside the area listening to the coach's instructions as he pretends to change channels on the TV. Each instruction has a simple movement to follow.

Examples of instructions: Fast forward = Move around the area; Slow motion = Players move in slow motion; Rewind = Players move backwards; Formula One = Players pretend to drive around the area in a racing car; Wimbledon = Players pretend to play a tennis match; Grand National = players pretend to be part of a horse race.

Coaching points: Encourage lots of movement. Spatial awareness – don't crash into other players in the area and look for the big spaces. Listening skills.

Progressions: Coach makes up more commands. Add a ball per player.

session 13 foxes and farmers

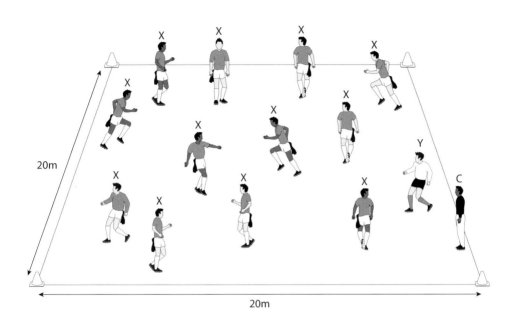

Organisation: Set out a 20 x 20m area. Select one player (Y) from the group to be 'the farmer' while the rest are 'foxes'. Each fox takes a bib and places it into the waistband of their shorts, hanging down like a tail.

Equipment: Bibs, marker cones.

Description: When the coach shouts go, the farmer chases the foxes around the area, trying to pull off their tails. If the tail is pulled out, the fox is out of the game. The last remaining fox is the winner.

Coaching points: Look around so you don't bump into anyone or run out of the area. When the farmer chases you, turn around to face him so it is more difficult for the farmer to pull the tail out.

Progressions: Start the game with two farmers. When a fox loses their tail they become a farmer.

session 14 cat and mouse

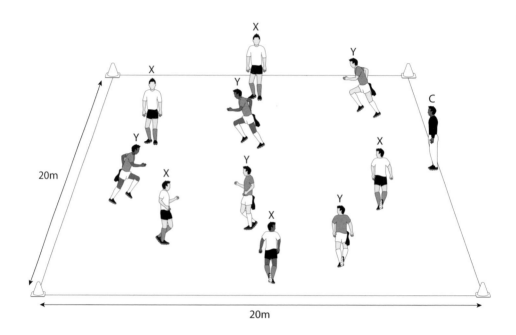

Organisation: Set out a 20 x 20m area. Play 5 v 5 inside the area. Each player from the 'mice' (Y) team takes a bib and places it into the waistband of their shorts, hanging down like a tail.

Equipment: Bibs, marker cones.

Description: The 'cats' (X) chase the mice (Y) around the area, trying to pull out their tails. Once the tail is pulled out both the cat and the mouse are out of the round until all mice are caught. Both teams play as cats, with the coach timing both teams to see which is the faster.

Coaching points: Work as a team to catch the mice. Use body swerves to lose the cat. When the cat chases you, turn around to face him so it is more difficult to pull the tail out.

Progressions: Give both teams a time limit of 30 seconds. Create an overload for the mice. Play 4 mice v 6 cats making it more difficult for the mice.

session 15 around the world

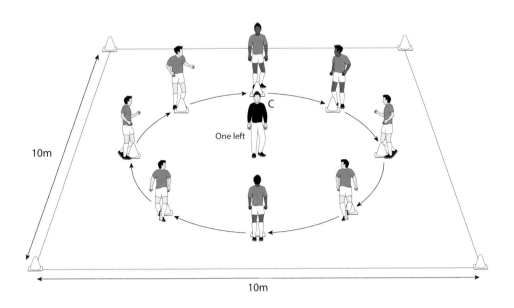

Organisation: Set out a 10 x 10m area. Set out a circle inside the area with marker cones, size will depend on the number of players. One player stands behind each cone, at least 5yd away from each other.

Equipment: Marker cones, footballs.

Description: The coach calls out a series of commands that relate to movements, making them more and more difficult each time. For example, one left = move to the cone to your left; one left, one centre, two right = one to the left, in and out to the centre, then two right.

Coaching points: Be on your toes, ready to move. Use your listening and reaction skills.

Progressions: Introduce more complicated combinations. Introduce different movements – forwards, sideways, backwards etc. Each player uses a ball and dribbles while completing each combination.

session 16 cone raider

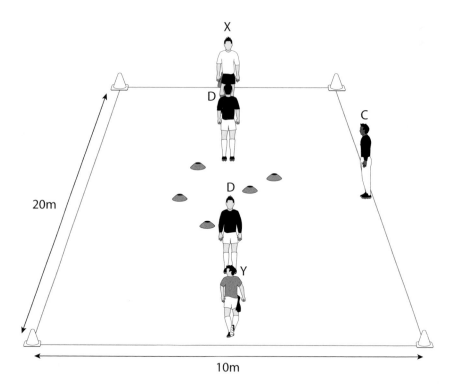

X

D

C

D

20m

Y

10m

Organisation: Set out a 10 x 20m area with five marker cones scattered in the centre of the area. Players X and Y take a bib each and place it into the waistband of their shorts, hanging down like a tail. Create sufficient areas for the number of players. Add two defenders to protect the cones in the centre of the area.

Equipment: Bibs, marker cones.

Description: Player X plays against player Y. On the coach's command they try to steal a cone from the centre of the area, one cone at a time per player. The defenders try to defend the cones, by attempting to pull out the tail of the X or Y player. If the tail is pulled out, the attacking player (X and Y players) starts again. Play until all the cones have been collected – whichever player has the most cones is the winner.

Coaching points: Use body swerves to lose the defender. Check in and out to make space for movement. The defender needs to stay low and side on.

Progressions: Play with two attackers (X and Y) against one defender (D), with 10 cones scattered in central area. Play with two attackers against two defenders, with 9 or 11 (odd number) cones scattered in central area. Play with a time limit, with the winner being the player who collects the most cones within the time limit.

session 17 here, there and everywhere

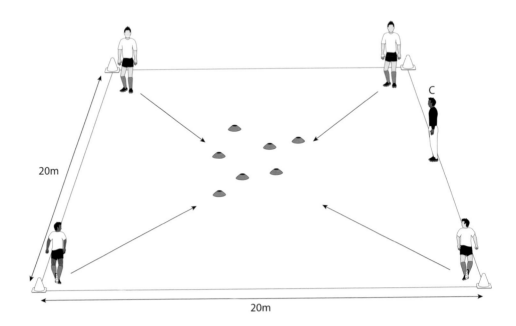

Organisation: Set out a 20 x 20m area, with one player in each corner and seven cones in the middle of the square. Create sufficient areas for the number of players.

Equipment: Marker cones, footballs.

Description: When the coach shouts 'Go!' the four players race to collect the cones from the centre of the square and return them to their corner – but they can only take one cone at a time. Once all the cones have gone from the middle the players may steal cones from each other's corners. The first player to collect three cones is the winner. Players cannot defend the cones in their corner, but must try to steal quicker than their opponents.

Coaching points: Use your speed to collect the cones quickly. Play with your head up so you can see who you need to steal from to prevent an opponent winning the game.

Progressions: Use nine cones; first to collect four is the winner. Replace the cones with footballs; players now dribble a football back to their corner before turning to look for another ball – players may not tackle one another while they are dribbling, only steal from the corners. Play in pairs, taking alternate turns to collect a cone/ball.

session 18 shopping list

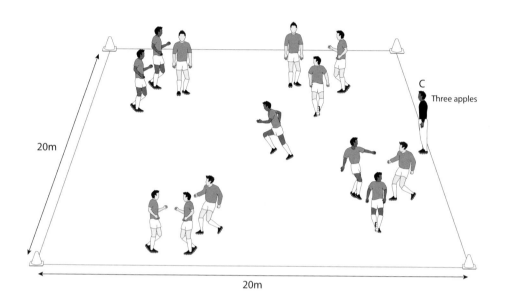

Organisation: Set out a 20 x 20m area. All players stand in a space in the area.

Equipment: Marker cones.

Description: The players start moving around in the area. The coach calls out his shopping list and any time he mentions a number the players get into a group of that number of people as quickly as possible, e.g. 'I went to the shops and bought three apples' means players get into a group of three. Any player not in a group of the right amount does a fun forfeit.

Coaching points: Move around the whole area. Players move in and out of the spaces created by the movement, not in a circle. Be aware of other players and spaces.

Progressions: Change movements to skipping, moving forwards or backwards, or moving side-to-side. Coach tells stories of his shopping list when he bought two apples and two bananas meaning players get into a group of total items bought: e.g. a group of four.

session 19 tag squares

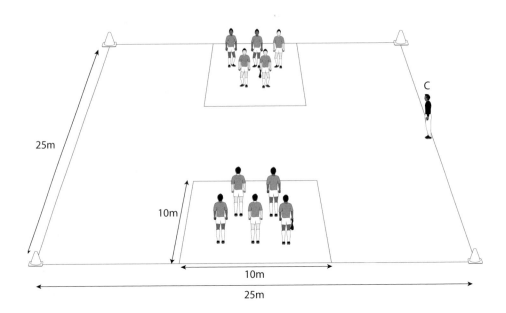

Organisation: Set out a 25 x 25m area, with two smaller 10 x 10m squares at either end. Players are separated into two groups and are positioned one group in each square.

Equipment: Bibs, marker cones, footballs.

Description: One player from the group in each square holds a bib and tries to tag another player. If a player is tagged, they take the bib and become the 'tagger'. When the coach calls 'Go', the players race to swap squares – with the last player to get to the other square becoming the 'tagger'.

Coaching points: Use body swerves to stay away from the tagger. Use clever movement to avoid the tagger. Use your speed so you are not the last player to the other square.

Progressions: Add an extra tagger. Change the type of movement between squares—backwards, sideways, skipping. Give each player a ball, with the tagger trying to win a ball from the other players instead of trying to tag them.

session 20 flip it, flop it

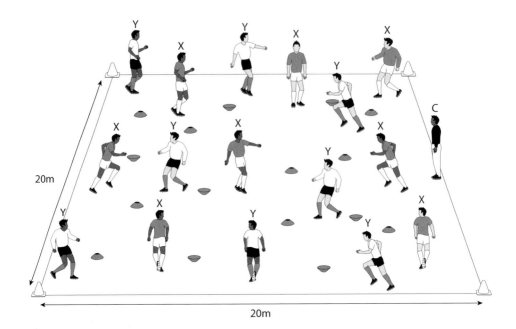

Organisation: Set out a 20 x 20m area and divide the players into two groups. Give each group an equal number of cones and tell one group to set out cones as 'flop it' (right way up, large base to the ground). Ask the other group to set out cones as 'flip it' (wrong way up, small top to ground).

Equipment: Bibs, marker cones.

Description: One group tries to turn the cones over one way – 'flip it', the other the opposite way – 'flop it'. Play for 90 seconds – whichever team has flipped or flopped the most cones wins!

Coaching points: Encourage players to look around to see which cones need to be flipped or flopped. Encourage positive and quick decision making. Communication – ask the players waiting for their turn to point out the cone that need to be flipped or flopped. Teamwork.

Progressions: Reduce the number of cones. Reduce the time limit to make this a quick reaction activity. Extend the time limit to make this an endurance activity.

FUN FOOTBALL GAMES

In this section you will find games that range from very easy and simple techniques to more challenging practices for advanced players. These sessions are designed to be simple to execute and fun in practice for both coach and player.

The more basic games in this section serve as a great platform for players who are starting out in football, while the more advanced sessions are designed to put players to the test to help them to develop as a player.

Regardless of the level of difficulty, the aim of each game is to engage the player's imagination and enthusiasm for football without focusing too heavily on technique – in other words, guided discovery over mundane line drills.

Working with a ball per player is essential in developing close control and helps promote the player's level of individual ball skills.

session 21 old macdonald

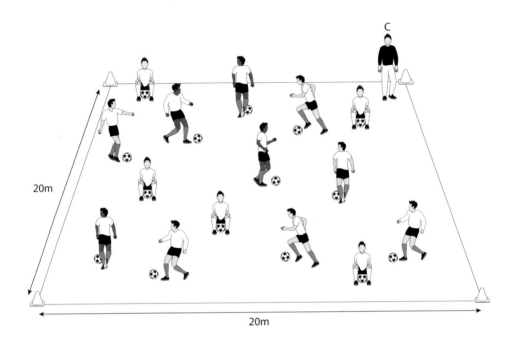

Organisation: Set out a 20 x 20m area. Players are randomly spaced in the area with one ball per player.

Equipment: Bibs, marker cones, footballs.

Description: Players dribble around the area. The coach leads them in the chorus of 'Old MacDonald Had a Farm'. When the coach gets to 'on the farm he had some...' he comes up with the name of a different animal each time. The players have to do the animal impersonation – with actions!

Examples of instructions: 'Chickens' = sit on the ball; 'frogs' = put the ball between your knees and jump around; 'pigs' = push the ball around the floor with your head; 'rooster' = move the ball around with your elbows (like wings); 'elephant' = move the ball around with your imaginary trunk (arm); 'seal' = try to balance the ball on your nose and make a noise like a seal.

Coaching points: Keep the ball close to your feet. Keep looking up and around. Do the impressions yourself so that they are properly demonstrated to the players.

Progressions: Dribble only using your weaker foot. Add a 'wolf' that comes to the farm to steal the balls.

>>> 27 – 30 – 77 – 91

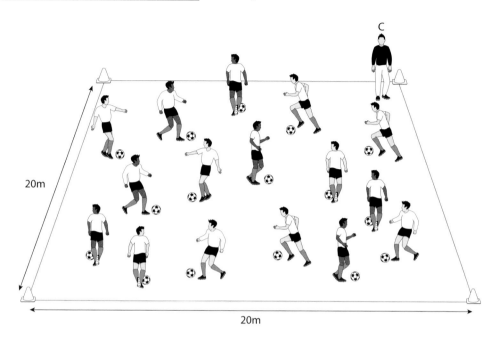

20m

20m

Organisation: Set out a 20 x 20m area. Players spread out inside the area, one ball per player.

Equipment: Bibs, marker cones, footballs.

Description: Players dribble their ball around in the area. As the coach calls out a body part, the players stop the ball with that part of the body. For example, if the coach calls 'knee' the players have to stop the ball with their knee, if the coach calls 'elbow' the players have to stop the ball with their elbow, if the coach calls 'head' the players have to stop the ball with their head. Try to come up with some more difficult parts of the body to stop the ball with, such as ear, shin, chest or nose.

Coaching points: Keep the ball close to feet while dribbling. Look up and around between touches. Use both feet. Use turns and changes of direction.

Progressions: Make it into a competition: slowest player is out of the game. Players use the specific body part to dribble the ball. For example, if coach calls 'knees', players have to dribble the ball with their knees for 30 seconds. Introduce a 'passive' defender to add pressure – a passive defender adds pressure by closing the ball down and restricting space, but not actually tackling the players or stealing the ball.

>>> 28 – 32 – 68 – 78

session 23 shadows and chasers

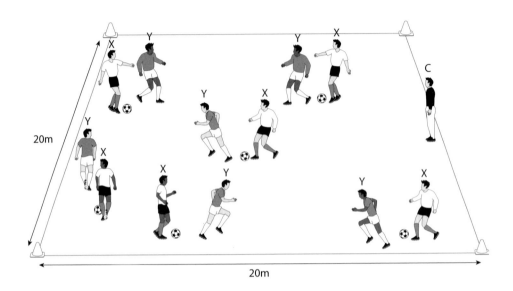

Organisation: Set out a 20 x 20m area. Set players out in pairs with one ball per pair.

Equipment: Bibs, marker cones, footballs.

Description: Player X starts with the ball. Player Y (their partner) runs around the area trying to stay as far away as possible from player X, who chases after them while dribbling the ball. When the coach shouts 'Freeze!' all players stop and stand still. Player Y then turns to face their partner, and player X attempts to pass the ball through their legs. Players then switch roles.

Coaching points: Keep the ball close to the feet when dribbling. Look up and around between touches. Try to use the correct weight and accuracy each time you pass, using the inside of the foot.

Progressions: Use the weaker foot when dribbling. Use the weaker foot when passing the ball. Award points for each successful pass.

》》》 35 – 38 – 89 – 96

session 24 colour squares

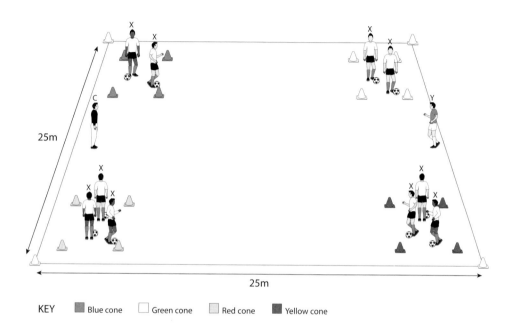

KEY ▪ Blue cone ☐ Green cone ▪ Red cone ▪ Yellow cone

Organisation: Inside a 25 x 25m area, mark out four different coloured smaller areas using marker cones. The X players have one ball each and dribble around the area, while a Y player is outside the area but cannot see the area (closes eyes).

Equipment: Marker cones, footballs.

Description: Coach gives the players inside the area a five-second countdown. During this countdown the players dribble around the area finding a square to stop in. The coach asks the Y player to call out a colour, and anyone inside that coloured square is out of the game.

Coaching points: Keep the ball close to the feet. Look up and around in between touches. Encourage positive and quick decision making.

Progressions: Change movements to each square (dribble, juggle the ball, left/right foot only). Limit players to a three-second countdown.

>>> 26 – 37 – 66 – 78

session 25 treasure hunt

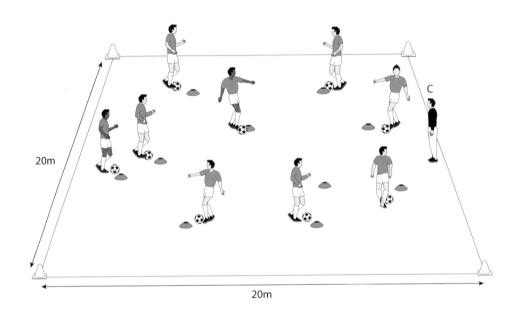

20m

20m

Organisation: Set out a 20 x 20m area. Place small cones randomly around the area. Each player plays inside the area.

Equipment: Bibs, marker cones, footballs.

Description: Players dribble around small cones that are scattered around the area. The object of the game is to pick up as many of the cones as possible while keeping the ball under control.

Coaching points: Keep the ball close to your feet. Take small touches. Keep your head up. Encourage spatial awareness (other players, other footballs and space within the area). Changing direction and turning with the ball.

Progressions: Restrict use of different feet (right foot only, left foot only). Alternate feet (use left foot, then right foot). Players have to balance cones on their heads as they collect them. Add a passive or active defender to pressure the ball – a passive defender adds pressure by closing the ball down and restricting space, but not actually tackling the players or stealing the ball, whereas an active defender is allowed to tackle and try to steal the ball.

>>> 36 – 46 – 81 – 90

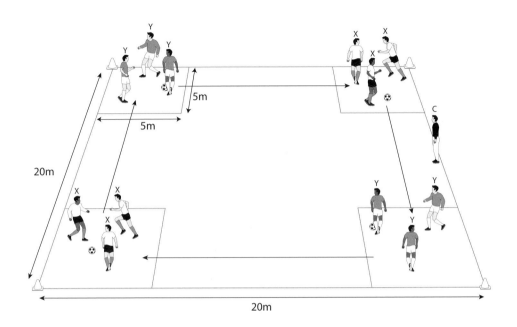

Organisation: Set out a 20 x 20m area with four 5 x 5m squares in each corner. Players are separated into teams of three and placed in each corner square. Each corner square is named after a famous football stadium.

Equipment: Bibs, marker cones, footballs.

Description: Players move around in the corner squares, dribbling their footballs. As the coach shouts 'Stadium swap!' the players have to run to the next stadium. Players move in a clockwise direction.

Coaching points: Players must move around their 'stadium' without bumping into each other. Keep the ball close to the feet while dribbling. Push the ball a little bit further out from the feet when travelling from one stadium to the next.

Progressions: Players dribble using weaker foot only. Use two balls between three players and have players passing the ball in the stadiums, running with the ball when they swap.

>>> 24 – 33 – 52 – 80

session 27 musical ball

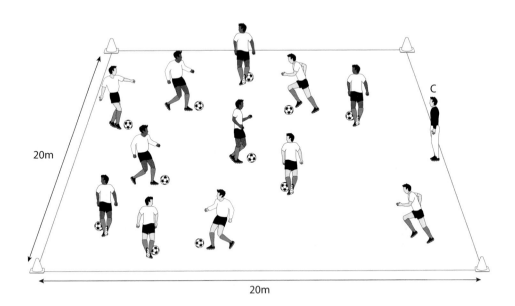

20m

20m

Organisation: Set out a 20 x 20m area. One ball per player, except for one player who starts without a ball.

Equipment: Bibs, marker cones, footballs.

Description: All players, except one, have a ball each and dribble around the area listening for the coach's commands. When the coach calls 'Change' all players leave their ball where it is and try to find a new ball. The player without a ball also tries to find a ball, leaving a different player as the 'odd man out'. This player then jogs around, and waits for the next 'Change' call from the coach to grab someone's ball.

Coaching points: Keep the ball close to the feet. Look up and around between touches. Use inside and outside of the foot, using both feet. Move to a new ball as fast as you can.

Progressions: Add the command of 'tap' where the player stops their ball, taps their foot on the top of another ball and then returns to their own ball. Have two players without a ball. Add turns (i.e. inside or outside hook) and moves to beat a player (i.e. step over or a shimmy) on different commands.

>>> 21 – 40 – 70 – 77

session 28 shark attack

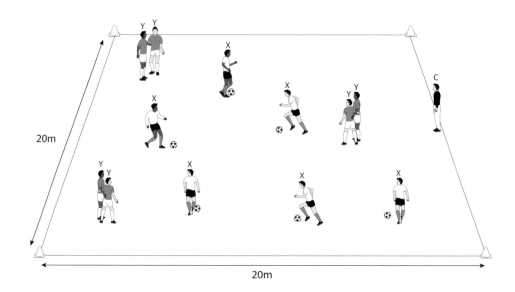

20m

20m

Organisation: Set out a 20 x 20m area. Y players act as defenders ('sharks') and are joined together, either holding a bib between them or by linking arms. X players have a ball each.

Equipment: Bibs, marker cones, footballs.

Description: X players dribble their ball around the area avoiding the Y pairs (sharks). If one of the Y pairs steals their ball they are out of the game and stand by the coach.

Coaching points: Look up and around between touches to see where Y players are. Keep the ball close to the feet and under control. Use turns and changes of direction.

Progressions: If an X player gets caught by a shark they leave their ball to the side of the area and join as an extra defender, helping the sharks to catch the remaining X players. Give sharks a ball between two, so they now have a ball to dribble while they move around, taking it in turns to dribble and direct.

>>> 22 – 32 – 62 – 91

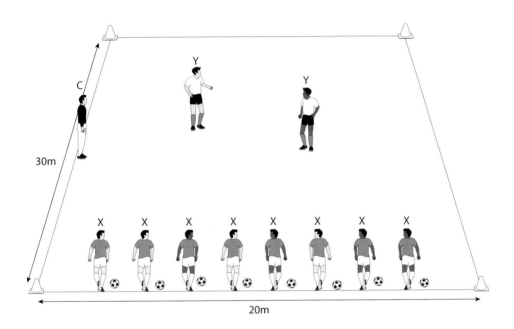

Organisation: Set out a 20 x 30m area. Two players are stationed in the middle of the area (Y) with the rest of the players (X) standing on the end line with a ball each.

Equipment: Bibs, marker cones, footballs.

Description: The two players (Y) are the crocodiles. The X players dribble their ball past the defenders to the other end line. Once they reach the end line they are safe and wait for the coach's command to try to get back to the other end line. If a crocodile manages to steal a ball, that player becomes a crocodile. The last X player left with a ball is the winner.

Coaching points: Keep the ball close to the feet while dribbling. Look up and around between touches while dribbling. Change direction to keep the ball away from defenders. Accelerate into spaces away from the defenders.

Progressions: Add extra defenders (crocodiles) after each round. Join the two defenders by holding a bib between them so they are connected and have to work as a team to steal the footballs.

》》》 23 – 28 – 64 – 83

session 30 strike out

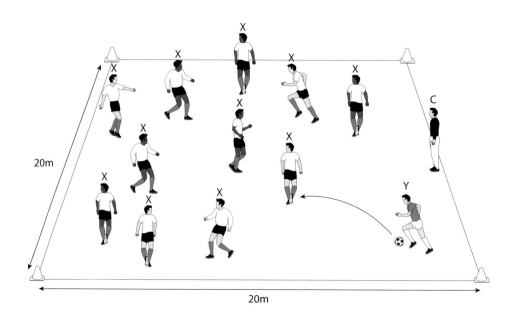

Organisation: Set out a 20 x 20m area. One player (Y) starts with a ball, the remaining players, without a ball, spread out inside the area.

Equipment: Bibs, marker cones, footballs.

Description: The Y player dribbles the ball around the area and attempts to hit the X players by passing the ball, aiming below the knee. Once an X player is hit, they get a ball and join the Y player.

Coaching points: Keep the ball close to your feet while dribbling. Dribble with your head up. Make accurate passes using the inside of the foot.

Progressions: Start the game with two Y players. Pass only with the weaker foot. Have one ball between two Y players so they pass to each other trying to strike out the X players.

>>> 27 – 39 – 44 – 85

session 31 dogcatcher

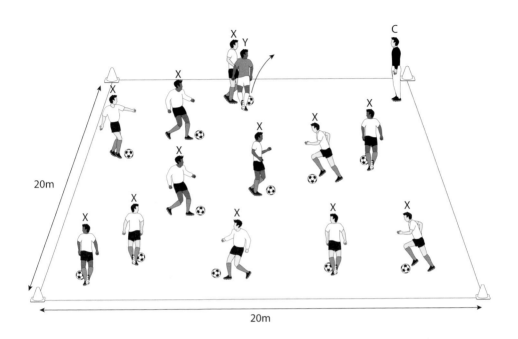

Organisation: Set out a 20 x 20m area. Select one player (Y) to be the dogcatcher. This player does not have a football. Everyone else (X) has one football and stands inside the area.

Equipment: Bibs, marker cones, footballs.

Description: On the coach's command the dogcatcher (Y) tries to kick everybody's football out of the grid. Whoever ends up as the last player remaining wins.

Coaching points: Keep the ball close to your feet. Use the inside of your foot. Be aware of footballs and players around you.

Progressions: Start the game with two dogcatchers. Players may only use their weaker foot. Players work in pairs, with one ball between two, trying to keep their ball away from the dogcatchers.

>>> 25 – 38 – 63 – 83

session 32   king of the ring

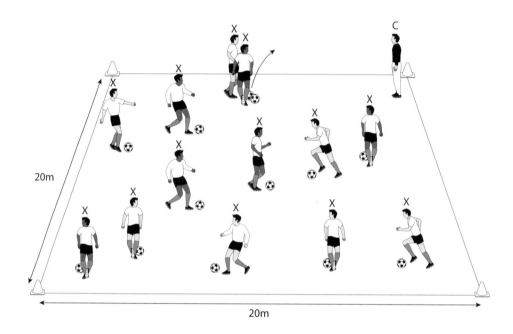

Organisation: Set out a 20 x 20m area. One ball per player. All players need to stay inside the area.

Equipment: Bibs, marker cones, footballs.

Description: All players (X) dribble around the area trying to avoid other players. If another player loses control of their ball or gets too close they can make a tackle and kick the ball out of the area. If a player's ball leaves the area they are out of the game.

Coaching points: Keep the ball close to the feet while dribbling. Look up and around between touches. Use turns, skills and changes of direction to move away from the defender (in progression).

Progressions: Start the game with one defender, who doesn't have a ball. Once their ball is kicked out of the area that player becomes a defender.

>>> 22 – 29 – 62 – 84

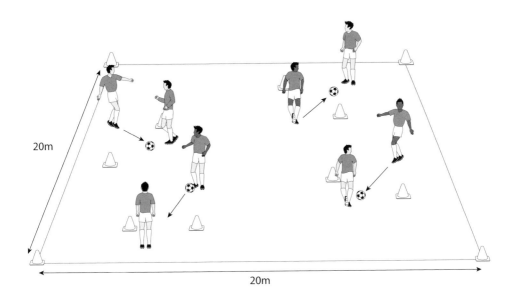

20m

20m

Organisation: Set out a 20 x 20m area. Set up small gates or goals using marker cones around the area, made up of two cones 3–5m wide. Players work in pairs, one ball for each pair.

Equipment: Bibs, marker cones, footballs.

Description: The players work in pairs, dribbling to each gate or 'goal'. As they arrive at a goal they must make five good passes (correct weight, inside of foot, not touching the gates on the way through) before moving to another goal. Only one pair can work at a goal at any time.

Coaching points: Pass the ball with the inside of the foot. Correct weight of pass – not so hard so it's too difficult for your partner to control, but not too soft so that the pass reaches your partner. Keep the ball close to your feet when dribbling to the next gate. Keep your head up so that you are aware of other players and empty gates. Communicate with your partner.

Progressions: Introduce a time limit. How many gates can you visit in 60 seconds? Have one pair of defenders in the area without a ball. Defenders try to steal the ball from the other players in the area. Make the gates smaller.

>>> 26 – 77 – 78 – 80

session 34 capture the flag

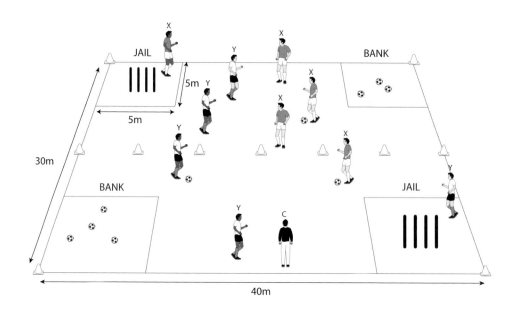

Organisation: Set out a 40 x 30m area. Divide the area into two halves with a centre line of cones. Mark 5 x 5m squares in each corner, one square in each half is the jail and the other is the bank. Place five balls in each bank.

Equipment: Bibs, marker cones, footballs.

Description: The idea of the game is for one team to collect all the footballs by invading the other team's half of the area, taking a football from their bank and dribbling it back to their own bank. Players are safe in their own half but if a player is tagged while in the opponent's half they must go directly to the opponent's jail. A player is released from jail only when a teammate crosses into the opposing half and high fives them. The first team to collect all of the balls wins.

Coaching points: Try to use both feet to dribble the ball. Keep your head up to look for space within the area. Work as a team. Communicate as a team.

Progressions: Allow teams to pass the ball to each other when stealing from the other team. Limit the number of players allowed in the opposition's half.

>>> 31 – 48 – 81 – 90

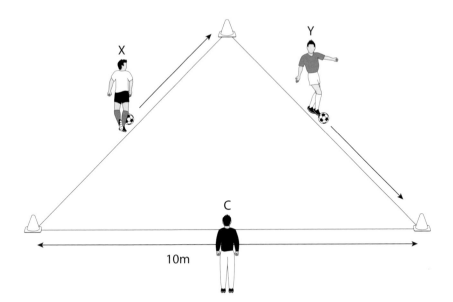

Organisation: Set out a triangle with each point 10m apart. Position two players on the outside of the triangle, with a ball each. Create sufficient areas for the number of players.

Equipment: Bibs, marker cones, footballs.

Description: While dribbling the ball player X tries to tag player Y by chasing him around the outside of the triangle. Player Y can dribble in either direction in order to lose his marker.

Coaching points: Keep the ball close to your feet to ensure it is under control. Dribble with your head up so you can see which direction your opponent is coming from. Use as many different types of turn as you can to change direction.

Progressions: Limit players to a specific type of turn, i.e. only an outside hook turn or only a drag back. Allow players to turn using only their weaker foot. The chasing player does not use a ball, making it harder for the dribbling player.

>>> 23 – 66 – 69 – 98

session 36 picnic basket

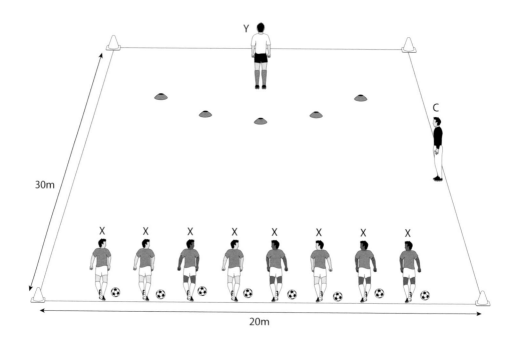

30m

20m

Organisation: Set out a 20 x 30m area. One player (Y) stands at one end of the area with his back to the rest of the players (X), without a ball. Place five cones (or more depending on size of group) behind Y. Each X player has a ball and a bib tucked into the waistband of the shorts like a tail.

Equipment: Bibs, marker cones, footballs.

Description: When Y has his back turned, the other players (X) start to dribble towards the opposite line, in order to try to steal a cone from behind the Y player. When Y turns around all the X players have to freeze – anyone caught moving gets sent back to the start line. Once a cone has been stolen, Y chases the X players back to the start line and tries to catch them by pulling out their tail. X players need to turn quickly with their ball and dribble past the end line to be safe.

Coaching points: Keep the ball close to the feet when dribbling. Turn quickly. Accelerate after turning. Push the ball a little further out from your feet when running with the ball.

Progressions: Gradually add more defenders (Y players). Allow Y players to tackle after a cone is stolen, instead of pulling out the tails.

>>> 25 – 35 – 52 – 88

session 37 steal ball

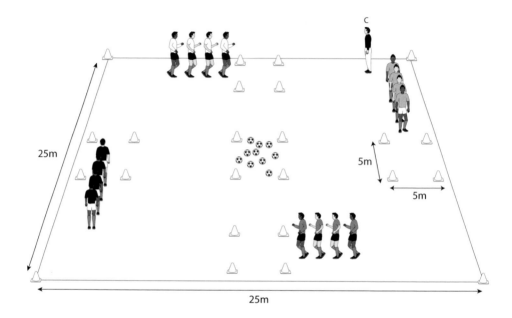

25m

5m

5m

25m

Organisation: Set out a 25 x 25m area, with a 5 x 5m square in the centre. On each touchline mark out four more 5 x 5m areas and place 16 footballs in the centre square. Put the players into four teams in each of the touchline squares.

Equipment: Bibs, marker cones, footballs.

Description: Like a relay race, when the coach shouts 'Go' the first member of each group runs out of their square and takes a ball and dribbles the ball back, then a teammate can go. The team with the most balls wins.

Coaching points: Keep the ball close to the feet when dribbling. Turn quickly. Accelerate after turning. Push the ball a little further out from your feet when running with the ball.

Progressions: Once all the balls are collected from the centre allow players to steal a ball from someone else's square – players must go through the middle square on the way there and the way back. Allow players to go two at a time.

>>> 24 – 60 – 69 – 97

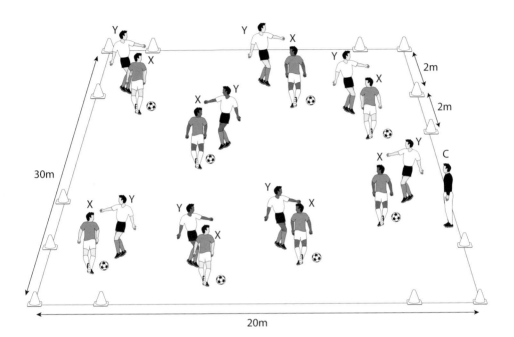

Organisation: Set out a 20 x 30m area. Players work in pairs, one ball per pair, and are stationed randomly within the area. Set up six small gates, two cones 2m apart around the outside of the area.

Equipment: Bibs, marker cones, footballs.

Description: X starts with the ball. The object of the game is to dribble through as many gates as possible in 2 minutes. The defender (Y) must attempt to dispossess the player in possession. If a player dribbles through a gate and stops the ball, score 3 points. Every turn or fake demonstrated scores 1 point. First player to 10 points wins. Once a goal is scored, the defender gets the ball. Players cannot go to the same goal twice in succession.

Coaching points: When the defender (Y) gets alongside (X), they should try to turn and go in a different direction. Make space, then accelerate away. Shield the ball and move into space away from the defender. Keep your head up and look around, so that you are aware of where the gates are.

Progressions: Develop into two teams with one ball. Two teams, but two balls in play.

>>> 31 – 63 – 99 – 100

session 39 hold that ball

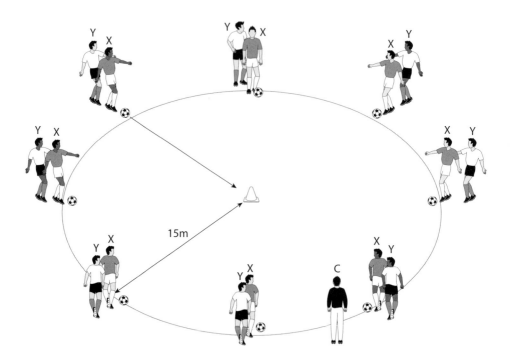

15m

Organisation: Set out a 30m diameter circle area with a central cone. Pairs (X and Y) stand 15m from the cone. Each pair has a ball. Create sufficient area for the number of players.

Equipment: Bibs, marker cones, footballs.

Description: X approaches the cone, does a turn then passes to Y. Y is told to 'hold the ball'. X then runs around behind Y, receives the ball back out in front and goes to the cone, completes another turn, and then dribbles back to Y. Repeat with Y now dribbling.

Coaching points: Dribble to the cone in the middle and turn quickly. Accelerate after the turn. Try to disguise the turn. After turning, get the ball out from under your feet.

Progressions: Instead of 'holding the ball', X dribbles to Y and plays a 1–2 pass. X then lets the ball roll through his legs, turns and dribbles to the central cone to do another turn. X dribbles the ball back to Y, plays a 1–2 pass but receives the ball after running around Y. Y has only one touch.

>>> 30 – 40 – 83 – 85

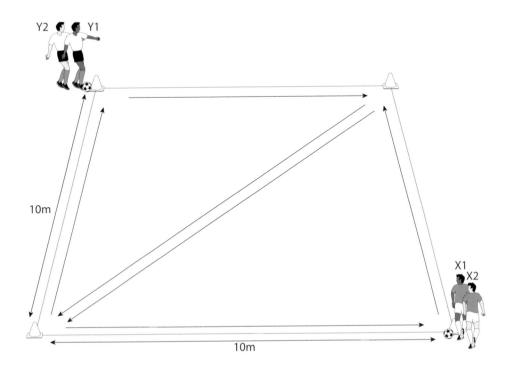

Organisation: Set out a 10 x 10m area, placing a cone at each corner of the square. Position two players at opposite corners of the area. Create sufficient area for the number of players.

Equipment: Bibs, marker cones, footballs.

Description: Players X1 and Y1 dribble to the cone, do a turn, sprint to the next cone, turn again and make a pass their partner.

Coaching points: Speed away from the cone – slow down towards the cone. Get low – have a wide stance. Get the ball out of your feet. Use a variety of turns: outside hook, inside hook, Cruyff turn, stop turn, step-over turn.

Progressions: Make it a race between X and Y player, where the quickest wins a point. Follow the pass to force X2 to get the ball out of their feet. Work both directions in order to practise with both feet.

>>> 37 – 39 – 76 – 90

session 41 tunnel pass

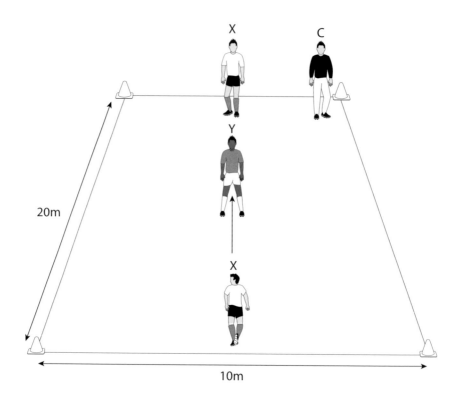

Organisation: Set out a 10 x 20m area. Position one player at each of the end lines of the area, and one player in the centre. Create sufficient areas for the number of players.

Equipment: Bibs, marker cones, footballs.

Description: The player in the centre stands with their legs open as wide as possible while the players at each end take it in turns to attempt to pass the ball through. A point is scored each time the ball is passed through Y's legs cleanly. First player to 5 points wins, then rotate players.

Coaching points: Pass using the inside of your foot. Correct accuracy and weight of pass – depending on the distance of your partner. Correct placement of your standing foot.

Progressions: Players can only pass using their weaker foot. Reduce the size of the passing gap. Increase the distance of the pass.

>>> 44 – 51 – 71 – 79

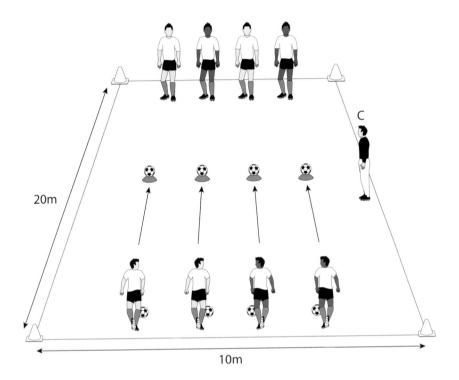

20m

10m

C

Organisation: Set out a 10 x 20m area. The players work in pairs on opposite sides of the area. In the middle of the area, in between each pair, place a marker cone with a ball balanced on top. Give a ball to each pair. Create sufficient areas for the number of players.

Equipment: Bibs, marker cones, footballs.

Description: The players pass the ball across the area with the aim of knocking the ball off their cone in the centre. Each player takes alternate turns with their partner with one point being scored for each time they knock the ball off the cone.

Coaching points: Pass the ball with the inside of your foot. Correct placement of your standing foot. Practice passing with both feet. Correct weight of pass.

Progressions: Each time the player knocks the ball off the cone, they take a big step backwards to increase the distance of the pass. Make the pass using the outside of the foot. Players work in pairs and combine their scores – first team to 10 wins.

>>> 52 – 79 – 81 – 87

session 43 first touch champion

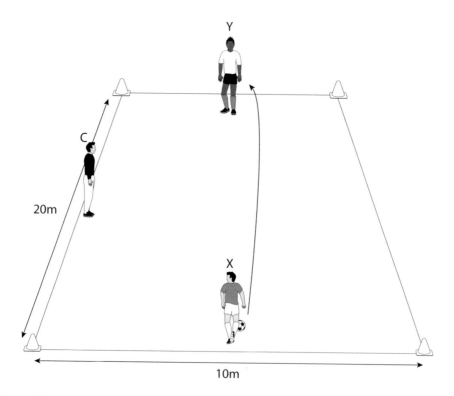

Y

C

20m

X

10m

Organisation: Set out a 10 x 20m area. One player starts at each end of the grid, one ball per pair. Create sufficient areas for the number of players.

Equipment: Bibs, marker cones, footballs.

Description: The object of the game is for each player to pass the ball past his or her opponent's baseline in order to score a point. The player at the opposite end tries to prevent the point being scored by stopping the ball before it crosses the line, but they may only use their feet. The ball must travel below waist height.

Coaching points: Pass using the inside of your foot. Control the ball with the inside of the foot, trying to 'kill' it so it doesn't bounce back to the other player.

Progressions: If player returns the pass and scores with their first touch they score two goals. Play using alternate feet to control and pass.

>>> 50 – 59 – 74 – 92

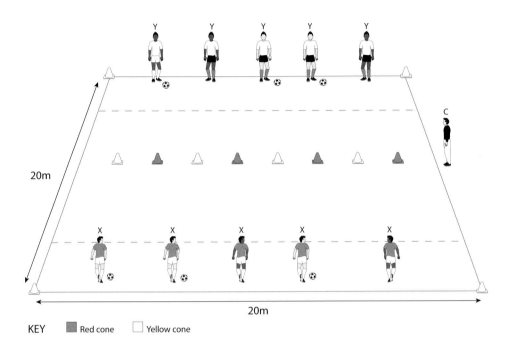

KEY   ▪ Red cone   ☐ Yellow cone

Organisation: Set out a 20 x 20m area, with different coloured cones lined across the centre. Split players into two teams who stand behind the baseline of each side of the area, facing the cones, with three or four balls per team.

Equipment: Bibs, marker cones, footballs.

Description: Players pass the balls trying to knock down the cones in the centre. X players aim for red cones, Y players aim for yellow cones. Players must stay behind the baseline when passing the balls but may move forward to collect another ball.

Coaching points: Make your pass as accurate as possible to knock down the cone. Pass the ball using the inside of your foot. Pass the ball along the baseline to get a better angle at a cone, encouraging teamwork.

Progressions: Pass the ball only using the weaker foot. Use different parts of the foot to strike the ball – inside, outside, laces. Increase the distance of the passes by moving the baseline further away from the cones.

>>> 41 – 45 – 72 – 94

session 45 non-stop bowling

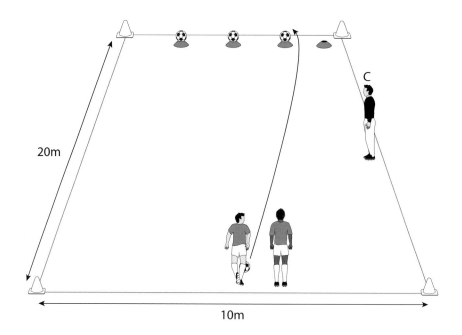

20m

10m

Organisation: Set out a 10 x 20m area. Repeat in other areas for correct amount of players. Station two players at one end with a ball behind a marker cone. At the other end of the area balance three balls on three cones and have another cone spare. Create sufficient areas for the number of players.

Equipment: Bibs, marker cones, footballs.

Description: Players work in pairs, taking it in turns to pass the ball, trying to knock the ball off the cone at the other end of the area. The player then retrieves the ball for their partner's turn. First pair to knock down their three balls wins the gold medal.

Coaching points: Use the inside of the foot when passing. Make your pass as accurate as possible to knock the ball off the cone. Use the correct weight of pass for the distance required. Correct placement of standing or non-kicking foot.

Progression: Once a ball has been knocked off a cone, the player may take the ball and place it on the spare cone of a different team. First team to have four empty cones is the winner!

>>> 41 – 42 – 82 – 89

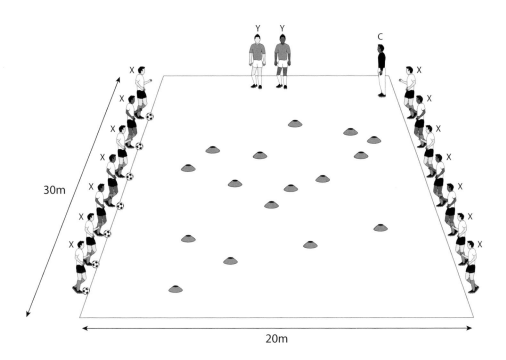

Organisation: Set out a 20 x 30m area. Players work in pairs. Station two players (Y) with a ball each at the baseline; the remaining pairs of players face each other on the sidelines, opposite their partner. Place cones randomly across the middle of the area.

Equipment: Bibs, marker cones, footballs.

Description: The Y players must dribble across the area without being hit on or below the knee by footballs which are being passed back and forth by the X players. Y players must attempt to pick up cones as they dribble across the area. Count the number of cones picked up in a 30-second period then rotate pairs so that everyone gets a turn to dribble and collect the cones.

Coaching points: Use the inside of the foot to pass the ball. Try to strike through the mid-line of the ball in order to keep the ball on the ground. Be aware of footballs and players around you.

Progressions: Pass the ball only using the weaker foot. Reduce the time limit to 20 seconds.

>>> 25 – 48 – 87 – 88

session 47 soccer squares

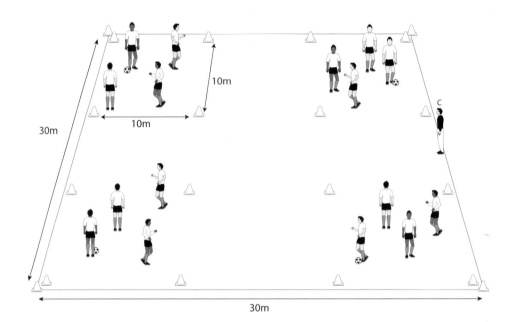

Organisation: Set out a 30 x 30m square, with a smaller 10 x 10m square in each corner. Each square has four players; each player is numbered one to four in each of their squares with one ball per square.

Equipment: Marker cones, footballs.

Description: The players pass the ball around within their square. On the coach's command the numbered players move clockwise to the next square, one at a time. For example, if the coach calls 'Number 1', all the number 1s move into the next square.

Coaching points: Encourage the players to communicate and call for the ball. Encourage players to move around as much as possible, no standing still. Use the correct passing technique.

Progressions: Limit players to two touches each time they receive the ball. The player entering the square must receive the ball straight away. Put a cone in the middle of the area; the players run to the cone then return to their original square.

>>> 26 – 71 – 75 – 93

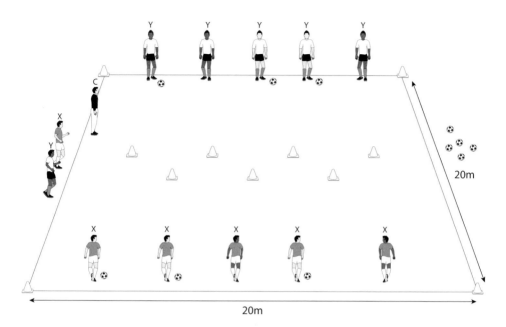

Organisation: Set out a 20 x 20m area. Players work in two teams, one team on each side of the area; a player from each team is stationed at the midway point at the side of the square. Five footballs are set up on the other side of the square opposite the players, also at the midway point. Place a number of cones across the middle of the area, staggered distances apart, to create a slalom.

Equipment: Bibs, marker cones, footballs.

Description: The two players to the side of the square run across the area, through the slalom of cones and collect a ball from the other side. They then have to dribble the ball back through the slalom to the start point. Meanwhile, the other team players are passing the balls across the square trying to hit the opposing players running across. The Xs are trying to hit the Y, and vice versa, to help their team. Players can only aim for below the knee. If they are hit they have to go back to the start point. The first player to collect three of the five balls is the winner.

Coaching points: Keep the ball close to your feet while dribbling. Try to make accurate passes using the inside of the foot. Look up and around to avoid other footballs.

Progressions: Dribble using one foot only. Pass with the weaker foot only. Player has to do kick ups on the way back through the slalom, keeping the ball off the floor.

>>> 34 – 49 – 80 – 97

session 49 soccer wars

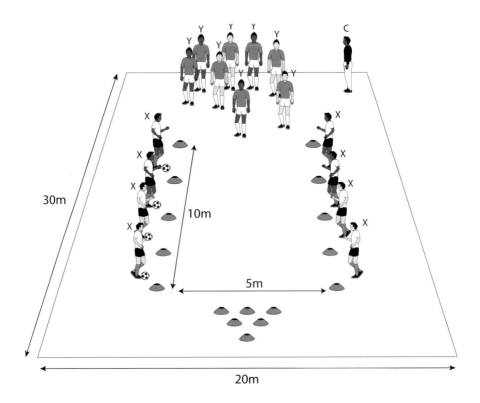

Organisation: Set out a 20 x 30m area. Place the cones in two rows, 5m apart and 10m long. Split the group into two teams (X and Y). X players are placed opposite each other, in between the two rows of cones and are given one ball between two while the Y players line up at the end of the area. Finally, place six cones at the other end to represent 'treasure'.

Equipment: Bibs, marker cones, footballs.

Description: X players pass the ball to their partner. On the coach's command, Y runs through the middle of the area and tries to return with one cone while trying to avoid getting hit on the knee or below. Once all Y players have been, X players try to beat their score.

Coaching points: Use the inside of the foot to pass the ball. Be aware of footballs and players around you. Correct placement of standing foot.

Progressions: Pass only using the weaker foot. The team collecting the cones can go two at a time, working in pairs.

>>> 41 – 75 – 82 – 100

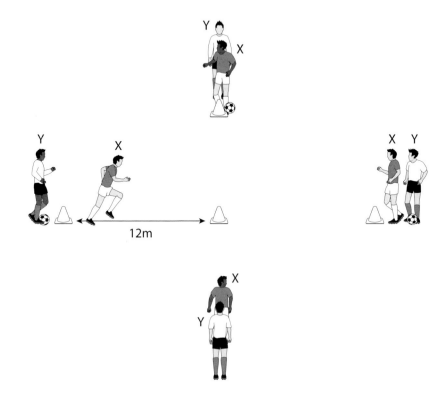

Organisation: Set out five cones in a cross formation 12m apart. Players work in pairs, the second player in each pair (Y) has a ball. Create sufficient areas for the number of players.

Equipment: Bibs, marker cones, footballs.

Description: On the coach's command, the X players race to the centre cone and then out to play a wall pass with each Y player, returning to the centre cone between each pass. The first player to get back to their start point having played four passes is the winner. Rotate players and keep scores.

Coaching points: Try to use the correct weight for the pass. Concentrate on the accuracy of passes. Call early for the ball. Use correct technique for first touch.

Progressions: Player Y starts with the ball in hands and serves underarm for a controlled volley return pass. Player Y starts with the ball in hands and serves underarm for chest or thigh control and a return pass. Player X starts with the ball, dribbles to the centre cone and turns each time, then plays a wall pass to player Y.

>>> 37 – 43 – 91 – 97

session 51 five and in

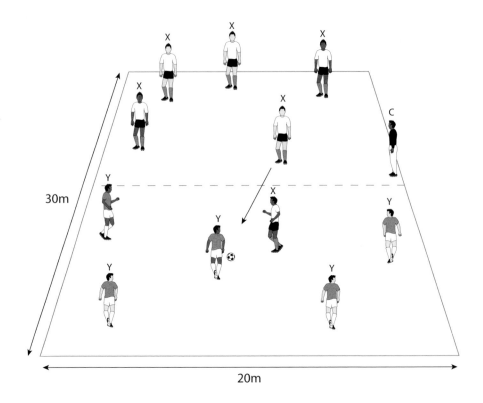

30m

20m

Organisation: Set out a 20 x 30m area with a centre line dividing the area into two halves. Arrange teams into 5 v 5.

Equipment: Bibs, marker cones, football.

Description: The attacking team (Y) spreads out, and plays 5 v 1 against the defender (X). After five successful passes the attackers score a point and another defender joins in. Continue until all the defenders are in play. If the ball is intercepted before five passes the teams swap roles. Whichever team scores the most points after five turns each is the winner.

Coaching points: Pass with the inside of the foot. Create an angle for the pass. Encourage positive and quick decision making. Communication: ask players to call for the ball. Teamwork.

Progressions: Make the area bigger (for defenders). Limit players to two or three touches (for attackers).

>>> 47 – 73 – 86 – 101

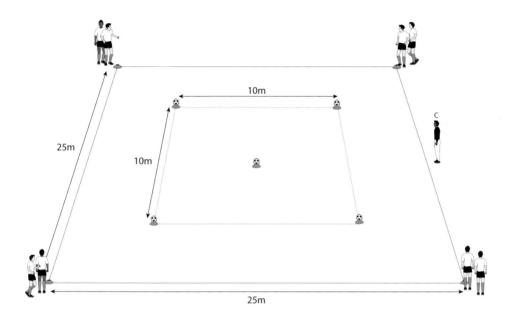

Organisation: Set out a 25 x 25m area, with a 10 x 10m square area inside. Place a football at each corner of the inner square and balance one on top of a cone in the centre. Position players in pairs or in small teams in the corners of the larger square.

Equipment: Bibs, marker cones, footballs.

Description: When the coach shouts 'Go!', the first player from each team races to complete a full circuit of the 'running track' – the area inside the large square, but outside the smaller one. When the player returns to the ball on their corner of the smaller square they pass it towards the centre aiming to knock the ball off the central cone. The first player to knock the ball off gets one point for their team. Rotate players and keep score.

Coaching points: Use the inside of the foot to pass the ball. Use the correct weight and accuracy for the pass. Keep the ball close to the feet when dribbling (during progression).

Progression: Players may only use their weaker foot to pass the ball. Players collect the ball and dribble around the running track then pass when back to their starting point. The coach calls 'Turn' as the players are dribbling around the running track and the player has to change direction.

>>> 36 – 42 – 59 – 83

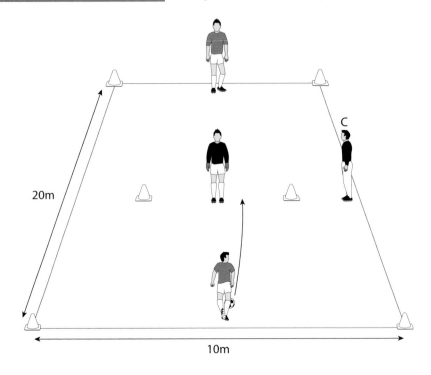

Organisation: Set out a 10 x 20m area. Two shooters are stationed one at each end of the area with a goal and a goalkeeper in the middle – the size of the goal should depend on the age and the level of ability of the players. Create sufficient areas for the number of players.

Equipment: Bibs, marker cones, footballs.

Description: The goalkeeper rolls the ball to one of the players at the end of the area who takes a touch to control then shoots at the goal in the centre. The player at the other end then takes a turn to shoot. Shooting players play head to head, first to 10 goals wins, and then rotate the goalkeeper.

Coaching points: Shoot using your laces. Try to hit the target (the goal). Aim for corners of the goal. Keep the ball low to make it difficult for the goalkeeper to make a save.

Progression: Allow shooters a one-touch rebound. Shooters must shoot first time from the goalkeeper's roll out. Award points for goalkeepers per save. Each time the shooter scores a goal they take one big step back, so they are further away from the goal.

>>> 55 – 61 – 94 – 95

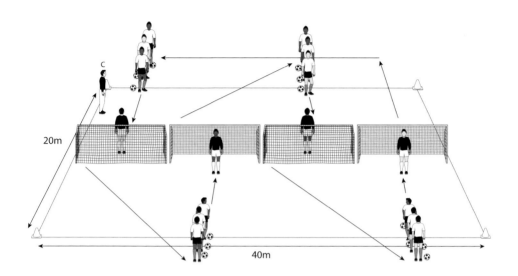

Organisation: Set out a 40 x 20m area with four goals positioned along the centre of the area, two facing each way. Select four players to be the goalkeepers and divide the rest of players into four groups, with each player being a striker (X).

Equipment: Bibs, marker cones, footballs, goals.

Description: On the coach's command X tries to score against the goalkeeper in front of them. After striking, the player takes the football and goes into the next position to take on the next goalkeeper. Everybody continues to shoot if the path in front of them is clear.

Coaching points: Shoot as quickly as possible. Shoot low and aim for the corners. Shoot hard using the laces. Observe the goalkeeper to see if he moves too early.

Progressions: Shoot with first touch. Use a shooting line (must shoot before you meet the line). Introduce a slalom before shooting. How many goals in a time limit.

>>> 53 – 57 – 64 – 86

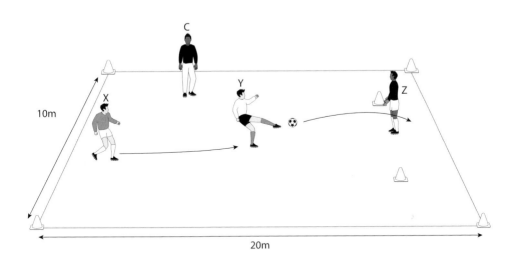

Organisation: Set out a 20 x 10m area. Players work in groups of three with three balls per group. Create sufficient areas for the number of players.

Equipment: Bibs, marker cones, footballs.

Description: X passes the ball to Y who turns and tries to shoot past Z. Player Y is allowed only three touches to score. See how many times a player scores out of three balls.

Coaching points: Try to hit the target. The receiver's first touch should be slightly angled to the side. Try to turn and shoot in one movement.

Progressions: The shooting player can only use the weaker foot. X now serves the ball with a throw in. Add a defender so the attacker has to turn, beat the defender then try to score.

>>> 53 – 58 – 65 – 96

session 56 goalie wars

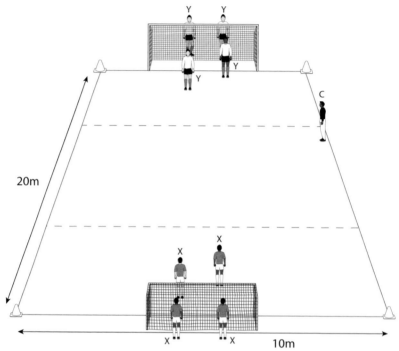

Organisation: Set out a 10 x 20m area. Organise players into two teams, with two players as goalkeepers and the remainder from each team lined up in pairs behind the goal at each end. Mark out a line of cones 5yd in front of each goal across the width of the area; creating two goalkeeper's areas and a middle area.

Equipment: Bibs, marker cones, footballs, goals.

Description: One player takes a shot, trying to score in the opposite goal. If they score they get one point but if the shot misses the target (i.e. goes wide or over) both players swap places with their teammates behind the goal. If the shot is saved by the opposition goalkeepers, play continues, with a player from that team taking a shot at goal. When a goal is scored, the two goalkeepers that concede the goal must change places with their teammates behind the goal. All shots must be taken from inside the goalkeeper's area; first team to 10 points wins the game.

Coaching points: Strike the ball with the laces. Throw the ball overarm (when progressed). Hit the target. Aim for the corners of the goal.

Progressions: Players may throw the ball overarm, or roll it underarm using goalkeeping techniques. Allow players to kick the ball from hands. Introduce the middle area as 'no man's land'. If the ball is in no man's land a player from either team may run in and take a first time shot.

>>> 54 – 70 – 88 – 92

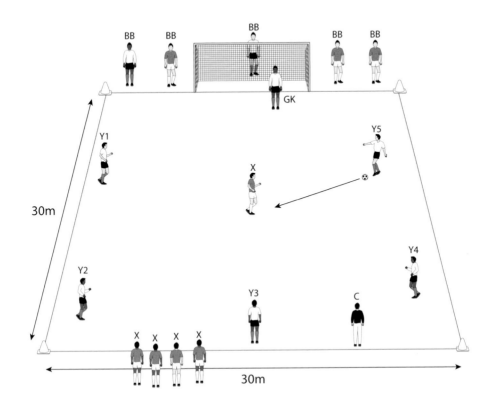

Organisation: Set out a 30 x 30m area. Select one player to be the goalkeeper (GK). Divide the rest of players into three groups; strikers (X), servers (Y) or ball boys (BB).

Equipment: Bibs, marker cones, footballs, goal.

Description: Each server (Y) has a number and as the coach calls a number, that player serves the ball into X who takes a touch and tries to score. Each X player takes a turn then all three teams rotate positions.

Coaching points: Shoot as quickly as you can. Shoot low and aim for the corners of the goal. Shoot hard.

Progressions: Shoot with the first touch. Add a defender to apply pressure to the shooter.

>>> 54 – 60 – 67 – 93

session 58 shooting stars

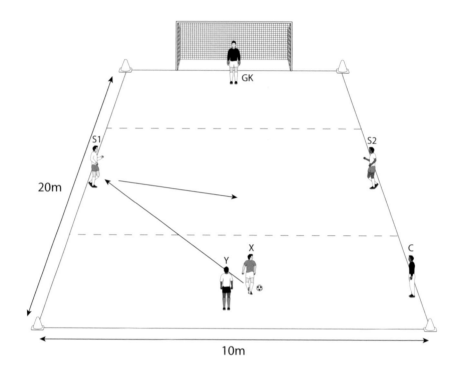

Organisation: Set out a 10 x 20m area. Add a goal and goalkeeper at one end. Organise two players (X and Y), who play head to head, and two servers (S1 and S2) to the side of the grid. Create sufficient areas for the number of players.

Equipment: Bibs, marker cones, footballs.

Description: Player X starts with a football and passes it to a server, either S1 or S2. The server then sets the ball back for player X who shoots at goal first time. Players X and Y take turns; first to five goals is the winner, then swap places with the servers.

Coaching points: Shoot using your laces for power. Shoot using your instep for placement. Aim for the corners of the goal. Keep your head over the ball.

Progressions: Shoot using weaker foot only. After the server sets the ball, the server on the opposite side moves to try to block the shot – applying pressure to the shooting player. Allow player Y to follow up any rebounds, making it a race to score the rebound.

>>> 55 – 61 – 69 – 86

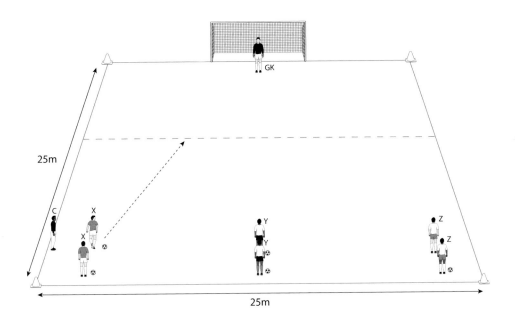

Organisation: Set out a 25 x 25m area, with three teams facing a goal, where each player has a ball. Create sufficient areas for the number of players. Mark out a line across the area as a shooting line. The distance of this line from the goal should depend on the age and level of ability of the group.

Equipment: Bibs, marker cones, footballs, goal.

Description: Player X dribbles their football to the shooting line and takes a shot at the goal, then turns to face player Y. Player Y plays a wall pass with player X, takes a shot at the goal, then turns to face player Z. Player Z dribbles their football and plays 1 v 1 against player Y, attempting to score a goal (player Z may score from past the line). Rotate player starting positions.

Coaching points: Shoot using your laces. Aim for the corners of the goal. Correct weight and accuracy of passes. Use skills, tricks and feints to beat the defender.

Progressions: Player X does a trick or a move to beat a player before shooting at the goal. Allow both Z players to play against player Y, creating an overload. Make the shooting line further away from the goal to encourage shots from distance.

>>> 43 – 52 – 70 – 96

session 60 football heaven

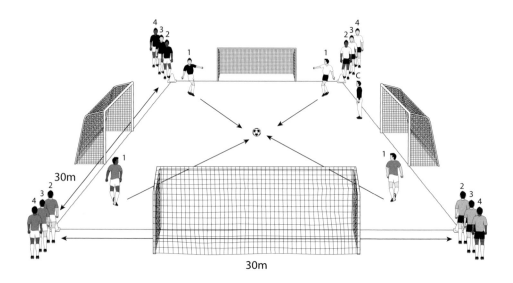

Organisation: Set out a 30 x 30m area with four goals placed along each touchline. Players are lined up at each corner and each player is given a number, i.e. 1–4, or 1–5 depending on number of players in each team.

Equipment: Bibs, marker cones, footballs, goals.

Description: When the coach calls out a number (e.g. 'Number 1') and serves the ball into the area. The players from each team with that number (e.g. of the four players, the one from each team who is numbered 1) enter the area and play against one another. The first player to score in any of the goals wins one point for their team.

Coaching points: Strike the ball with the laces. Be aware of players and the nearest goal to you. If a goal is blocked, use a turn to change direction and attack a different goal.

Progressions: Call out more than one number at a time. Reduce the number of goals on the pitch. Add a goalkeeper to each goal.

>>> 37 – 57 – 67 – 98

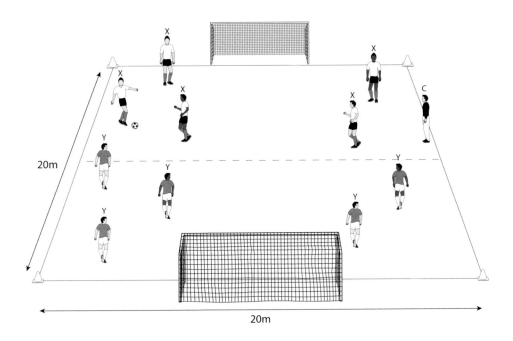

Organisation: Set out a 20 x 20m area, with a dividing line in the centre. Select two teams, with one on either side of the line.

Equipment: Bibs, marker cones, football, goals.

Description: Each team tries to score by shooting into the opposition's goal. Players must stay in their own half. No player is allowed to use his or her hands.

Coaching points: Shoot using laces for power. Try to make passes to teammates to set them up for shots.

Progressions: Make the goals larger to encourage success. Players have to shoot first time. Include a goalkeeper who may use their hands.

>>> 51 – 53 – 58 – 86

session 62 short, back and sides

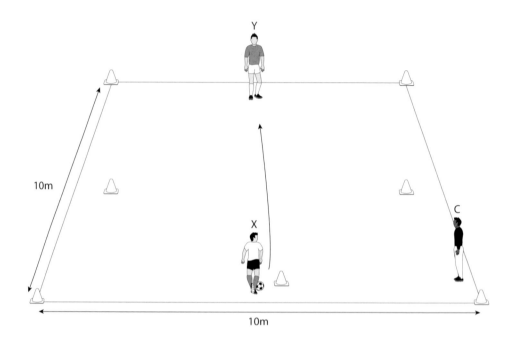

Organisation: Set out a 10 x 10m area. Players work in pairs with one ball per pair, one player positioned on each end line so that the players are opposite each other. Two cones are placed midway between the two players but 5yd wider to either side.

Equipment: Bibs, marker cones, football.

Description: X starts with the ball and passes it to Y. As soon as Y touches the ball, X leaves the cone they are standing at, and towards Y to try to win it back. Y tries to dribble to either of the two midway (wide) cones to score one point. If Y dribbles the ball around X to the cone at the other end (which X has just vacated), they score two points. Repeat the practice with X in possession.

Coaching points: Push the ball to the side and accelerate into space behind the defender. Change speed and direction. Use fakes and turns.

Progression: If the defender wins the ball, he becomes the attacker and tries to score.

>>> 32 – 65 – 77 – 80

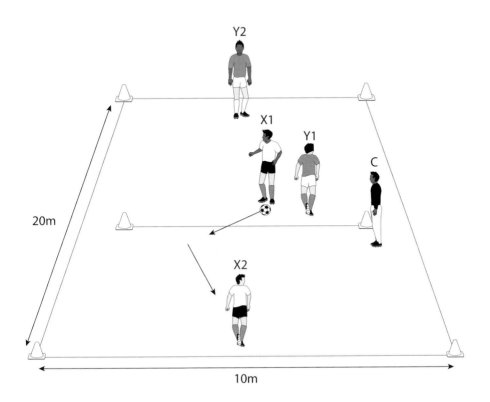

Organisation: Set out a 10 x 20m area. Players work in pairs with one ball per pair. Create a halfway line using cones. Create sufficient areas for the number of players.

Equipment: Bibs, marker cones, football.

Description: X1 starts with the ball and tries to beat defender Y1 by crossing the halfway line at the 10m marker. Once in the other half, X1 can pass to their teammate who is standing in the centre of the end line. If the defender (Y1) wins the ball, they can immediately attack the opposing half.

Coaching points: Attack the space to the sides of the defenders. Use your change of pace and change of direction to out-play your opponent. Once you make space, try to play the ball forward.

Progressions: Allow the end line players to move along the line to receive the ball. Allow attacking players to pass the ball from inside their own half.

>>> 31 – 38 – 66 – 78

session 64   1 on 1 with a goalkeeper

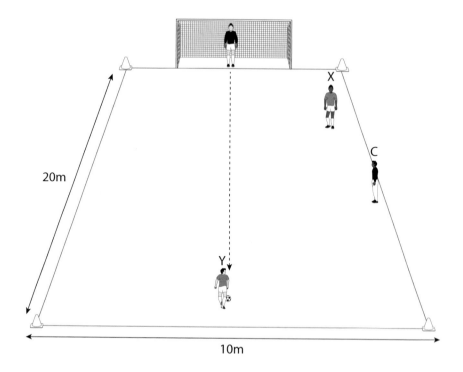

Organisation: Set out a 10 x 20m area with a goal positioned on the end line. Players work in groups of three, one ball per group. One player is the goalkeeper and stands in the goal, one player is a defender (X) and stands at a midway point to the side of the goal, and the third player is the attacker (Y) and stands at the baseline. Create sufficient areas for the number of players.

Equipment: Bibs, marker cones, football, goal.

Description: The goalkeeper starts with the ball and passes to Y who must attempt to dribble past X and score a goal. If the defender wins the ball, they should try to dribble over the end line. Play for five attacks then rotate positions.

Coaching points: Keep the ball close to your feet. Beat your opponent with a 'believable' trick. Make an early decision.

Progressions: Introduce more defenders. Reduce the space.

>>> 29 – 54 – 68 – 88

session 65 run the gauntlet

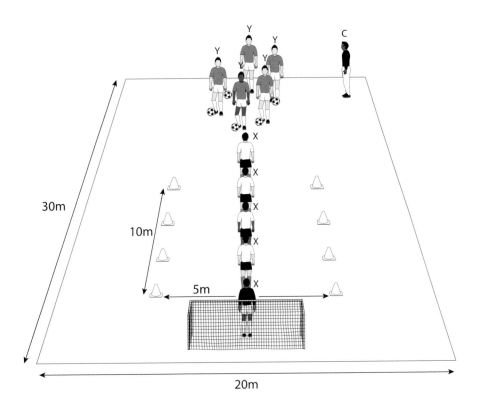

Organisation: Set out a 20 x 30m area and place two rows of cones 5m apart along a 10m length in the middle of the area, in front of a goal. Split the group into two teams (X and Y). The X players are placed in between the two rows of cones; they cannot move forwards or backwards, only sideways. A goalkeeper is in goal at the end of the grid. Y players are lined up with a ball each.

Equipment: Bibs, marker cones, football, goal.

Description: On the coach's command, Y tries to dribble past each defender (X) by using a trick. If Y manages to dribble past every defender they can try to score a goal. X players try to defend the goal by kicking the ball out of the area.

Coaching points: Keep the ball close to your feet. Make your move to beat a player (i.e. step over, feint) believable.

Progressions: Introduce more defenders. Reduce the defenders' space.

>>> 28 – 55 – 62 – 91

session 66 triangle goals

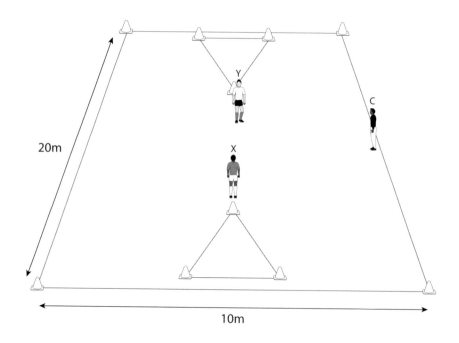

20m

10m

Organisation: Set out a 10 x 20m area. Using three cones create a triangle at each end of the area, each side approximately 3m long. Create sufficient areas for the number of players.

Equipment: Bibs, marker cones, footballs.

Description: Play 1 v 1. Players can score two ways: first, they can dribble into the triangle and stop the ball with the sole for two points. Secondly, they can pass the ball through the triangle for one point. First player to reach five points wins.

Coaching points: Encourage the players to use feints, step-overs and other moves to beat an opponent. Use the inside of the foot to make an accurate pass through the triangle. Move the ball quickly to create enough space to make the pass through the triangle.

Progressions: Add a player to each side to make the game 2 v 2. The ball has to be passed into the area with the teammate controlling the ball to score a point. Encourage movement off the ball.

>>> 35 – 63 – 40 – 85

session 67   1 v 1 with side-on goals

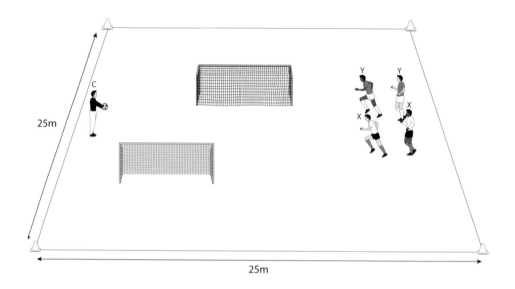

25m

25m

Organisation: Set out a 25 x 25m area, with two goals inside the area facing away from each other. Two teams line up to the side of the area.

Equipment: Bibs, marker cones, football, goals.

Description: As the coach rolls the ball into the area, one player from each team enters and they play 1 v 1. The first player to score in either goal is the winner, if the ball goes out of play, that game is over. Rotate players and keep score.

Coaching points: Shield the ball using your body to keep the ball. Use your dribbling skills to beat your opponent. If you can't score in one goal, use a turn to change direction and attack the other goal.

Progressions: Move the position of the goals. Play 2 v 2. Introduce a time limit to each game.

>>> 31 – 58 – 60 – 76

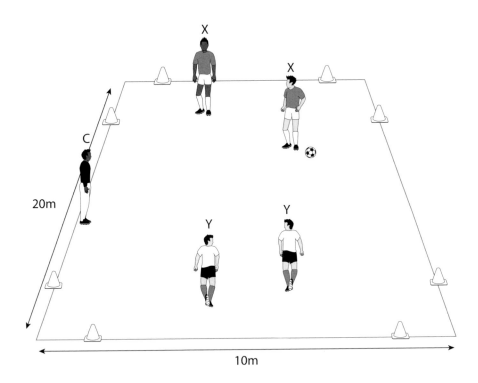

X

X

C

20m

Y

Y

10m

Organisation: Set out a 10 x 20m area. Play 2 v 2 with four small 'goals' placed in the corners of the area. Position the teams one at each end of the area, this will be the end line, which they defend.

Equipment: Bibs, marker cones, footballs.

Description: Teams play 2 v 2 and score points by stopping the ball on the opponent's end line for 1 point, dribbling through one of the small goals for 3 points or by using a move to beat a player then dribbling through a small goal for 5 points.

Coaching points: Encourage attacking play in 1 v 1 situations. Use fakes and moves to beat a player to get past the defender. Accelerate after a move to get away from the defender.

Progressions: Change to one small central goal to make it harder for attackers. Play with one player from each team man-marking the other

>>> 22 – 30 – 64 – 96

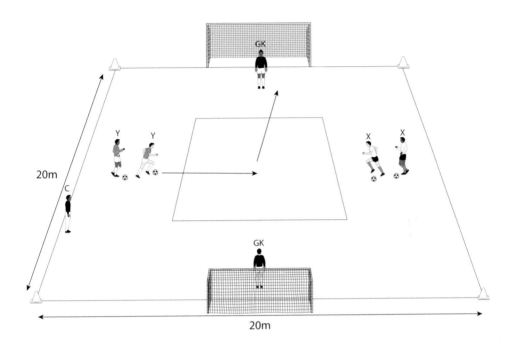

Organisation: Set out a 20 x 20m area, with a goal and goalkeepers at either end. Play with two teams, X and Y, which are stationed to the side of the area with a small square marked out in the middle. The size square should depend on the age and level of ability of the group but should be roughly 5 x 5m or 8 x 8m square.

Equipment: Bibs, marker cones, footballs, goals.

Description: Each player goes one at a time and makes a pass into the central square then follows their ball. With their second touch the player takes a shot at either goal before repeating from the other side of the square. X's play against Y's to see who can score the most goals in 5 minutes!

Coaching points: Correct weight and direction of the pass into the central square. Shoot using the laces and aim for the corners of the goal. Follow the ball in for rebounds.

Progressions: Shoot only with the weaker foot. Limit the amount of time. Allow a player from the other team to close the ball down and apply pressure to the shooting player.

>>> 35 – 58 – 70 – 94

session 70   3 v 2 defend and attack

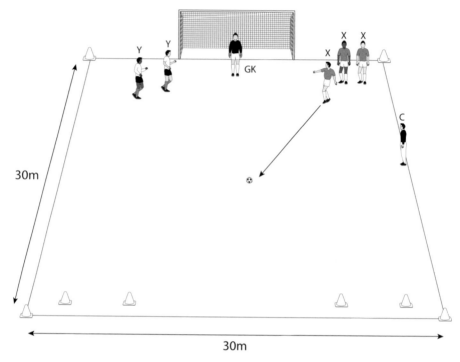

30m

30m

Organisation: Set out a 30 x 30m area, with one big goal at one end guarded by a goalkeeper and two unguarded smaller goals at the other end. Three attackers (X players) stand to one side of the goal, with two defenders (Y players) on the other side of the goal.

Equipment: Bibs, marker cones, footballs, goal.

Description: The goalkeeper starts with the ball and rolls it out into the field of play. The X players chase the ball, collect it, turn to attack the big goal and try to score. Once one of the attackers touches the ball, the Y players work as a pair to defend the big goal. If the Y players win the ball they can attack one of the two smaller goals at the other end, with the X players now defending the small goals.

Coaching points: Work as a team, creating space for a shot at goal. Encourage movement off the ball. Encourage positive decision making – when to pass, dribble or shoot.

Progressions: Ask the goalkeeper to throw the ball into different areas of the field (left, right, or centre) to encourage attacking from a different area of the pitch. Introduce a first time finish rule to encourage team play.

>>> 27 – 59 – 95 – 99

SMALL-SIDED FOOTBALL GAMES

Small-sided games are a developmentally appropriate environment for young players to learn and improve. Each game incorporates a specific football technique such as dribbling, passing or shooting, or focuses on team play and strategies such as defending, attacking, creating space or switching play. These games are specifically designed to bring the best out of players in realistic match situations. By allowing the players to enjoy more playing time, their understanding of the importance of team play, relative positional sense and decision making will be greatly improved.

The ability to control the ball with different parts of the body is a vital element in the modern game. Being skillful and having good close control in all areas of the pitch will separate the good players from the great players.

session 71 bingo

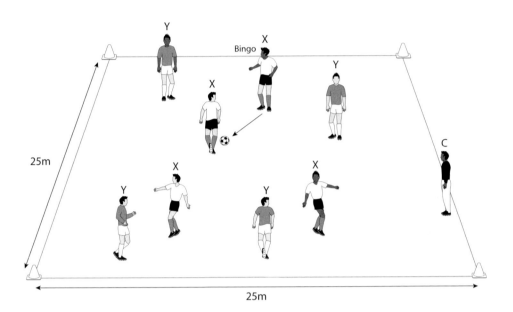

Organisation: Set out a 25 x 25m area, with teams set up 4 v 4.

Equipment: Bibs, marker cones, football.

Description: Teams play 4 v 4 inside the area but the players also work as individuals. Each time a player makes a successful pass they call out a number, 'one' for the first, 'two' for the second and so on. To win the game each player on each team must make 10 successful passes. When a player reaches 10 passes they shout 'Bingo!' then continue to play to help their teammates reach their targets.

Coaching points: Encourage plenty of movement to help the player on the ball. Players shout out their scores to encourage communication. Only successful passes count, so use correct weight and accuracy.

Progressions: Increase to 5 v 5 or 6 v 6. Increase number of passes to 15 or 20. Once a player reaches their target they are limited to two touches.

>>> 41 – 47 – 72 – 87

session 72 tag team

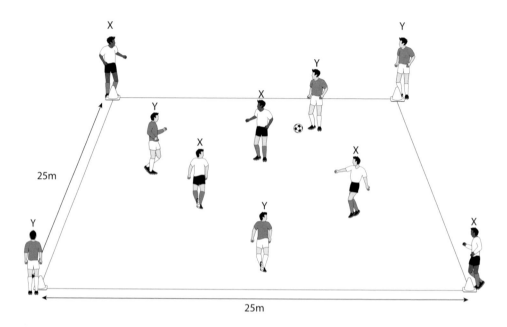

Organisation: Set out a 25 x 25m area. Two teams of five play 3 v 3 in the centre and the other two players on each team are positioned at opposite corners of the area. Create sufficient areas for the number of players.

Equipment: Bibs, marker cones, footballs.

Description: Teams play 3 v 3 inside the area, and are allowed to tag in and out of the game with their support players on either corner, at any time. The first team to make 10 successful passes gets a point.

Coaching points: Move around to create space for your team. Use dribbling skills to keep the ball for your team when under pressure. Use support players tactically, tag out when you get tired, tag back in when you are trying to keep the ball.

Progression: The two outside players become support players to make a 5 v 3 when in possession. Limit players to two touches. Allow support players to move along the outside line of the area.

>>> 44 – 49 – 74 – 101

KEY ■ Red □ Yellow ■ Blue ■ Green

Organisation: Set out a 50 x 40m area. Arrange players into four equal teams, one team with yellow (Y) bibs, one with red (R) bibs, one with green (G) bibs and one with blue (B) bibs.

Equipment: Bibs, marker cones, footballs.

Description: The object of this game is to keep the ball between two teams – red and yellow play together, against blue and green. Once a player wins possession yellow and red work together to try to keep the ball away from blue and green, however, red players may only pass to yellow and vice versa. Same rule applies for blue and green. The first two teams to make 10 consecutive passes win the game.

Coaching points: Encourage movement off the ball. Look up and around to ensure you pass the ball to the correct team. Encourage communication between the two teams. Each player's first touch should take him or her into a space, away from a defender.

Progressions: Limit players to two touches each time they receive the ball. Introduce neutral players (with no bib), who play for whichever team has possession of the ball. Introduce a target player at each end line; a point is scored when a team manages to pass the ball to one of these target players.

>>> 47 – 51 – 82 – 92

session 74 keep two balls

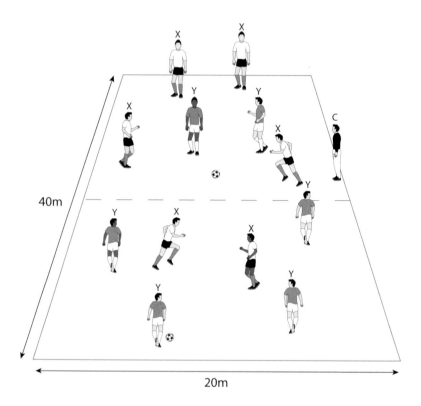

40m

20m

Organisation: Set out a 20 x 40m area with a central dividing line to create two 20 x 20m areas. Play 4 v 2 on each side of the centre line with one ball on each side.

Equipment: Bibs, marker cones, footballs.

Description: The four players (X) in each area pass the ball to each other aiming to keep possession and the ball away from the two defenders. If the defenders (Y) win the ball, they try to pass it across the centre line to their teammates on the other side where they continue to play 4 v 2 but with two balls.

Coaching points: Encourage teamwork – attack as a team and defend as a team. Try to make accurate passes with the correct weight. Ask players to communicate and call for the ball.

Progressions: Limit players to three or two touches each time they receive the ball. Play with four balls, starting with two balls in each area.

>>> 43 – 50 – 72 – 98

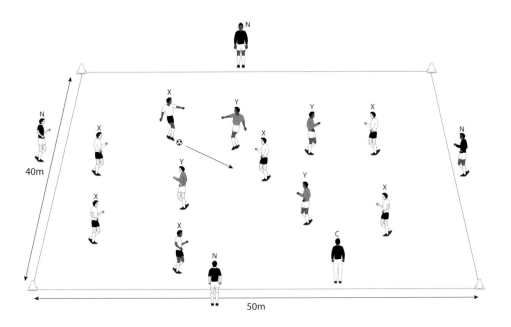

Organisation: Set out a 50 x 40m area. Organise seven X players against four Y players with four neutral (N) players on each side of the area, who act as support players and play for whichever team has possession of the ball.

Equipment: Bibs, marker cones, footballs.

Description: X players start with the ball: the aim is to keep possession in an 11 v 4. Once the Y players win the ball it will create an 8 v 7 scenario. X players need to make 10 consecutive passes for a point, while Y players only need to make five.

Coaching points: Encourage movement off the ball. Encourage teams to communicate and call for the ball. Take your first touch away from a defender and into space. Ask the defending team to pressure the ball in pairs.

Progressions: Limit the X players to two touches each time they receive the ball. Every time the ball goes out, re-start with the X team.

>>> 47 – 82 – 87 – 99

session 76 directional play

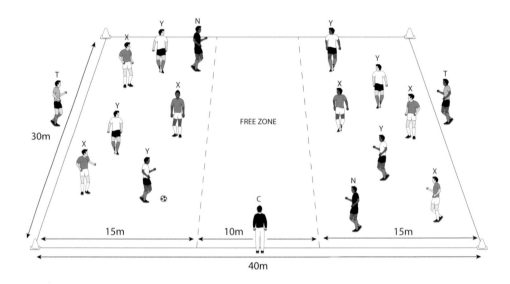

Organisation: Set out a 40 x 30m area split into three sections – two 15m sections either side of the central 10m section, the free zone. Two teams (X and Y) play 3 v 3 in each end area. One football is in play.

Equipment: Bibs, marker cones, football.

Description: The aim is for the X players in one area to pass the ball to their fellow X players in the opposite area; the passes go through the 'free zone'. No players are allowed to enter the free zone. Y players do the same when they are in possession. The N players are neutral and play for whichever team has possession of the ball, to create an overload of 4 v 3.

Coaching points: Encourage movement off the ball. Encourage players to communicate and call for the ball. Ask players to concentrate on the quality of their first touch.

Progressions: Add a target player at each end, the aim now is to pass the ball from your end area, into your teammate's at the other end and then to the target player to score. After scoring with one target player you must score in the opposite end. Introduce a minimum number of passes before you can score.

>>> 40 – 50 – 79 – 93

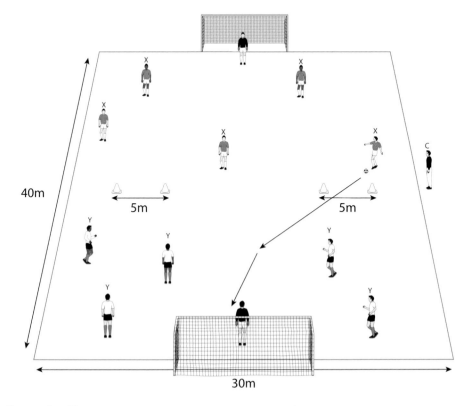

Organisation: Set out a 30 x 40m area, with two 'gates', 5m wide at the midway point and at either side of the area. Organise two teams, X v Y.

Equipment: Bibs, marker cones, football, goals.

Description: Teams must pass the ball through a gate before they can score a goal, but if they lose possession they have to go through the gate again. They may go either way through the gate.

Coaching points: Encourage players to pass the ball. Encourage players to create space in order to receive the ball. Ask players to communicate with each other and call for the ball.

Progressions: The team must play through both gates without losing possession to score. Players must dribble through the gate instead of making a pass.

>>> 21 – 62 – 68 – 80

session 78 four corners

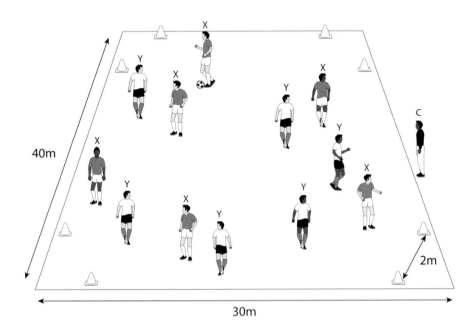

Organisation: Set out a 30 x 40m area with four small goals (approx. 2m apart) placed diagonally in each corner. Teams play 6 v 6 with no goalkeepers.

Equipment: Bibs, marker cones, football.

Description: X's play 6 v 6 against Y's, with the aim of dribbling the ball through one of the corner goals to score a point. Players can attack any goal while in possession.

Coaching points: Players should try to create space so that teammates can score in the wide areas. Try to get the ball wide. Switch the point of attack where possible.

Progressions: Teams cannot score in the same goal twice in a row. Teams only attack the two goals at one end/side of the area. Teams only attack diagonally opposed goals.

>>> 24 – 33 – 60 – 77

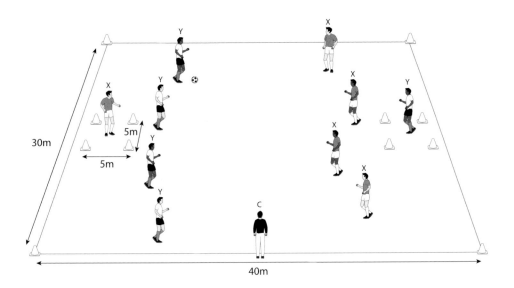

Organisation: Set out a 40 x 30m area with a 5 x 5m target area at each end. Organise the players into two teams – one player from each team stands in the target area.

Equipment: Bibs, marker cones, football.

Description: Each team has to score by passing the ball to their player in the target zone. Once a goal has been scored, the player who made the successful pass changes places with the target player. No one is allowed in the target area except the target player.

Coaching points: Encourage teamwork. Make accurate passes with the correct weight. Ask players to move in order to create space. Encourage positive and quick decision making.

Progressions: Pass to target player has to be a first-time pass. Limit all players to two touches, each time they receive the ball. Put a player from each team in a larger area to try to defend the target player. Pass has to be lofted so that the target player catches it.

>>> 42 – 45 – 76 – 101

session 80 gate crasher

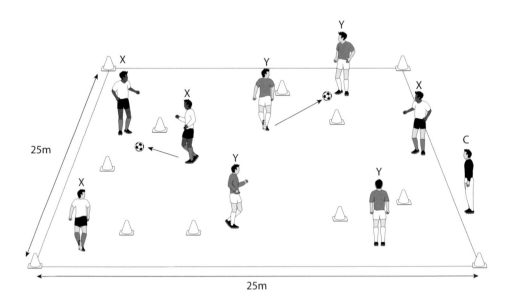

Organisation: Set out a 25 x 25m area. Five cone 'goals' (or gates) are spread out throughout the area.

Equipment: Bibs, marker cones, footballs.

Description: Teams play 4 v 4 inside the area. To score a goal, a successful pass must be made through any of the gates and controlled by a teammate on the other side, and play continues. The first team to score five goals wins.

Coaching points: Use the inside of the foot to make accurate passes. Encourage players to move off the ball to create space. Use dribbling skills to keep possession for your team.

Progressions: Teams cannot score in the same gate twice in a row, encouraging changing the point of attack. The pass through the gate has to be a first-time pass. Limit the players to three or two touches.

>>> 26 – 66 – 77 – 85

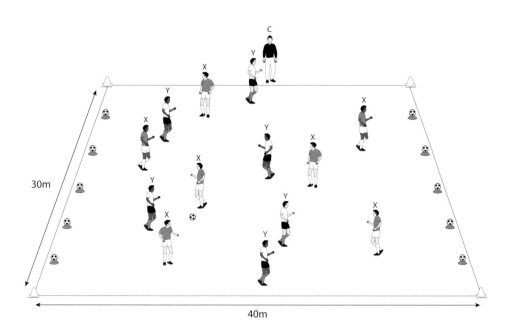

Organisation: Set out a 40 x 30m area. Place five cones on the end line with a football balanced on top of each. Organise two teams playing 5 v 5 or 6 v 6.

Equipment: Bibs, marker cones, footballs.

Description: The object of the game is to score a point by knocking one of the balls off a cone on your team's attacking end line. The first team to knock all the balls off the cones wins the game.

Coaching points: Encourage the players to shoot at the target whenever possible. Pass the ball, and then move into space. Try to pass the ball forwards and between defenders.

Progressions: Players can only score with a first-time pass. Players can only score with their weaker foot. Limit players to two or three touches.

>>> 25 – 42 – 45 – 89

session 82 support play

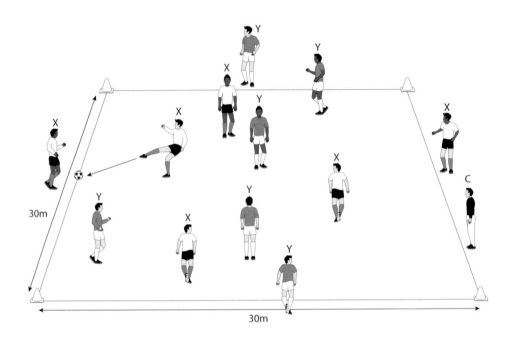

Organisation: Set out a 30 x 30m area. Play 4 v 4 inside the area and station two support players per team outside the area as shown in the diagram.

Equipment: Bibs, marker cones, football.

Description: Teams play 4 v 4 inside the area. A point is scored when a team passes the ball to one of their support players outside the square. The support players can move along their sideline of the area. First team to score 10 points wins.

Coaching points: Encourage team play and passing. Try to play to the support player as quickly as possible. Open play up by receiving on the 'half turn', using your back foot to control the ball.

Progressions: Teams have to play to both support players to score a point, encouraging switching of play. The player who passes to the support player then swaps places, making the play more continuous. Limit players to two touches.

>>> 49 – 74 – 75 – 97

session 83 · wembley way

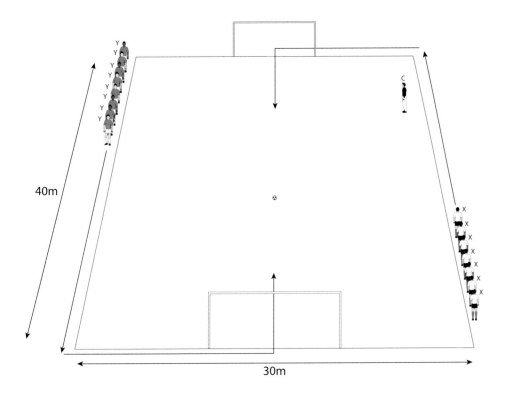

40m

30m

Organisation: Set out a 30 x 40m area with a goal at each end. Position players in two rows on each side of the area as shown in the diagram; each player is given a number.

Equipment: Bibs, marker cones, footballs, goals.

Description: As the coach calls out a number, the player from each team with that number runs around the outside of the field and through their goal and on to the field of play. The coach serves a ball into the middle of the area. Players must compete to win the ball and attempt to dribble or shoot the ball into the goal.

Coaching points: Keep the ball close to your feet when dribbling (1 v 1). Shoot using your laces for power. Use your dribbling skills and moves to beat a player (i.e. step-overs and changes of direction) to beat your opponent. Work as a team (during 2 v 2 or 3 v 3 progression)

Progressions: Call more than one number at a time, creating 2 v 2 or 3 v 3 games. Introduce a first-time finish rule to encourage team play.

>>> 39 – 64 – 65 – 84

session 84 — 4 x 4 golden goal

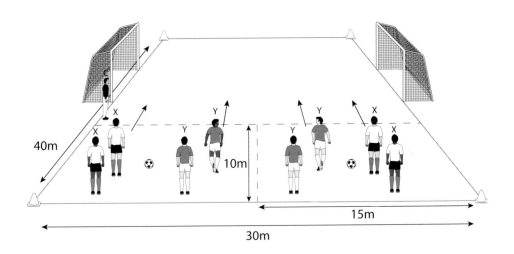

40m

10m

15m

30m

Organisation: Set out a 30 x 40m area, with two 15 x 10m areas on one side.

Equipment: Bibs, marker cones, footballs, goals.

Description: Teams play 2 v 2, keeping possession in the two smaller areas (X v Y). When the coach shouts 'Change!' all players move quickly to the larger area as a 4 v 4 trying to attack the opposition goals, no goalkeepers. During the 2 v 2, five consecutive passes make 1 point. During the 4 v 4 the first goal wins, then players return to the 2 v 2 grids.

Coaching points: In 2 v 2, work hard to make spaces for a pass. In 2 v 2, keep the ball for your team by using close control, individual skill and by shielding the ball. In 4 v 4, play positive (attack minded) football to attack the goal to score the 'golden goal'. In 4 v 4, get players behind the ball and defend as a team.

Progressions: Introduce a first-time finish rule to encourage build-up play. Play the best of three goals in the larger area. Add goalkeepers.

⟩⟩⟩ 29 – 36 – 63 – 83

session 85 | five-goal football

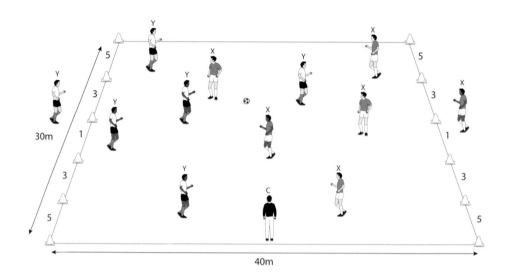

Organisation: Set out a 40 x 30m area with five small goals placed along the goal line. Play 5 v 5 with one player from the opposing team floating behind the goal line.

Equipment: Bibs, marker cones, football.

Description: Play X's v Y's, 5 v 5, inside the area. To score points players pass the ball through one of the small goals so that their teammate, floating behind the goals, can control the ball. Which small goal the ball is passed through will dictate how many points that pass scores, as shown in the diagram. The player who passed the ball now swaps places with the player behind the goal line.

Coaching points: Players should try to create space so that teammates can score in the wide areas. Try to get the ball wide. If one side is congested, try to switch the point of attack.

Progressions: Limit players to two or three touches. Add a defender to the float player area to try to cut out scoring passes.

>>> 30 – 33 – 77 – 80

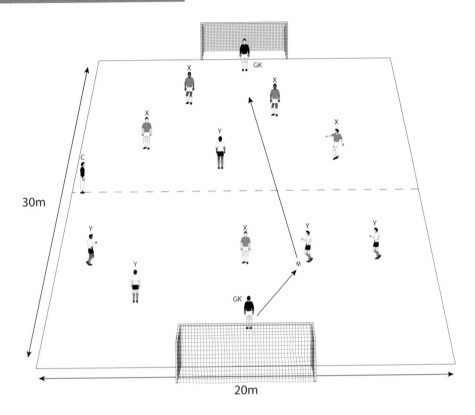

30m

20m

Organisation: Set out a 20 x 30m area. Play 5 v 5 with a 4 v 1 and a goalkeeper on each side of the dividing centre line.

Equipment: Bibs, marker cones, footballs, goals.

Description: The goalkeeper starts with the ball and gives it to any of the players on their team in their half of the pitch. They then shoot at the goal at the other end of the area from inside their own half. The opposing players try to block the shot and the lone player in the other half tries to convert any rebounds. Players must stay in their own half at all times.

Coaching points: Use laces when shooting. Aim for the corners of the goal. Follow in for rebounds. Shoot as soon as an opportunity arises.

Progression: Make five passes in your own half under pressure from the one defender before you can shoot.

>>> 54 – 56 – 61 – 95

session 87 lumberjacks

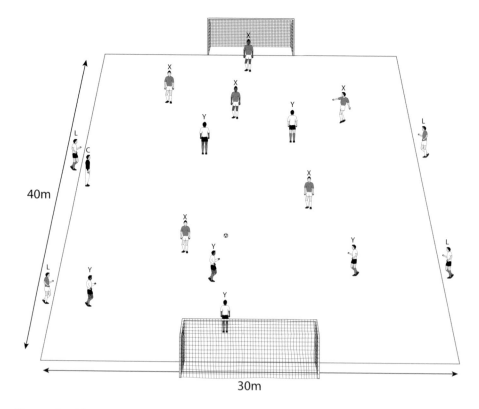

40m

30m

Organisation: Set out a 30 x 40m area. Play 5 v 5 with goalkeepers and station two 'lumberjack' (L) players on each touchline of the area.

Equipment: Bibs, marker cones, football, goals.

Description: Play as a normal 6 v 6 but instead of the ball going out for a throw-in, players can use the lumberjack players on the sidelines to keep the ball in play. Lumberjacks can move up and down the touchline and play for whichever team is in possession to provide width.

Coaching points: Get the ball wide. Play to lumberjacks on both sides, switching the point of attack. Defend as a team when not in possession as an attacking overload is created.

Progressions: The ball has to be passed to a lumberjack on each side before players can attack the goal, encouraging switch of play. A goal can only be scored from a cross or pass provided by a lumberjack. Limit all players except lumberjacks to two touches.

>>> 44 – 46 – 75 – 82

session 88 switch soccer

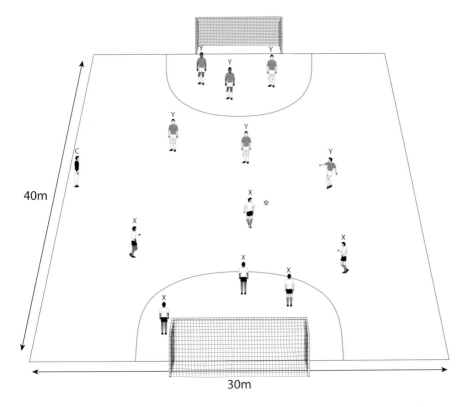

Organisation: Set out a 30 x 40m area, with a goal area marked as a 'D'. Play 6 v 6 with three players in the goal area and three players outfield.

Equipment: Bibs, marker cones, footballs, goals.

Description: Play 3 v 3, with three goalkeepers only allowed in the goal area. Goalkeepers may not use their hands. Whenever the coach calls 'Switch' the three goalkeepers switch places with the three outfield players and the game continues.

Coaching points: Defend the goal as a team. Shoot at goal whenever you have the chance. Encourage players to make space by going wide and deep.

Progressions: Limit the outfield players to two or three touches. Allow goalkeepers to use their hands. Develop into a 6 v 6 match.

>>> 39 – 62 – 70 – 96

session 89 touchdown

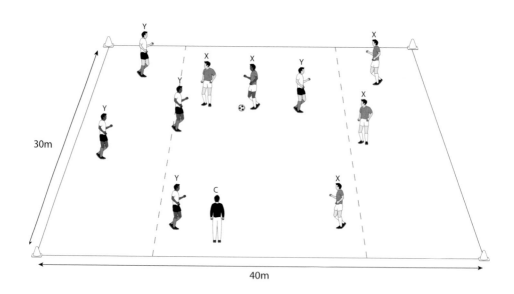

30m

40m

Organisation: Set out a 40 x 30m area, with a touchdown zone at each end 10m from the goal line.

Equipment: Bibs, marker cones, football.

Description: To score a point, players have to dribble into their opponent's end zone and stop the ball under their foot.

Coaching points: Encourage teamwork and passing. Ask players to move off the ball in order to create space. Encourage positive and quick decision making.

Progressions: Limit players to two touches each time they receive the ball. Add a permanent defender in the end zone to guard the defensive area. Players cannot dribble into the area but must make a run into the area and then receive a pass from a teammate.

>>> 22 – 43 – 79 – 81

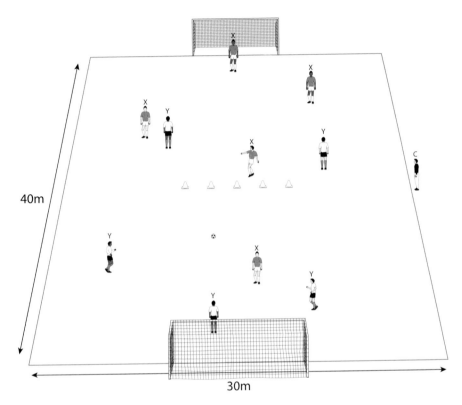

Organisation: Set out a 30 x 40m area. Place a line of marker cones across the centre of the area, creating a wall.

Equipment: Bibs, marker cones, football, goals.

Description: Teams play 5 v 5, trying to score in the opposition's goal. During play the ball is only allowed to travel around the outside of the wall and not the centre of the area. Players are allowed to run through or over the cones, but the ball must travel around the outside of the line marked with cones.

Coaching points: Get the ball wide. Switch the play in order to attack from both sides of the field. Be patient and composed in possession – wait for an opportunity to open up.

Progressions: Allow players to make lofted passes over the cones to reach the wide players. Decrease the number of cones until you can play a small-sided game without the wall.

>>> 25 – 34 – 82 – 100

session 91 breakout

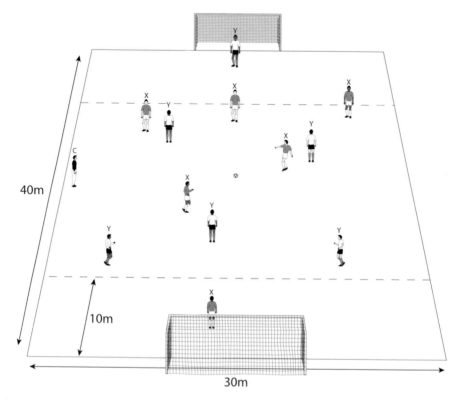

40m

10m

30m

Organisation: Set out a 40 x 30m area with goalkeeper zones 10m from each goal line. Play 5 v 5 in the middle area with one goalkeeper at each end.

Equipment: Bibs, marker cones, football, goals.

Description: Play as a 5 v 5 trying to score in the opponent's goal. A team can only score if one of their players dribbles the ball into the goalkeeper's area where they go 1 v 1 against the goalkeeper. No defenders are allowed in the area. Goals can only be scored in the end area.

Coaching points: Play as a team, spreading wide and deep to create space in the central area. Try to stay composed when 1 v 1 and attacking the goalkeeper. Aim to place the ball into the corners away from the goalkeeper.

Progressions: Attacker is limited to three touches when they enter the end zone. Allow one defender into the end zone to put extra pressure on the attacker. Attacker may only have a one-touch rebound if the goalkeeper makes a save.

>>> 28 – 55 – 64 – 83

session 92 twenty-ones

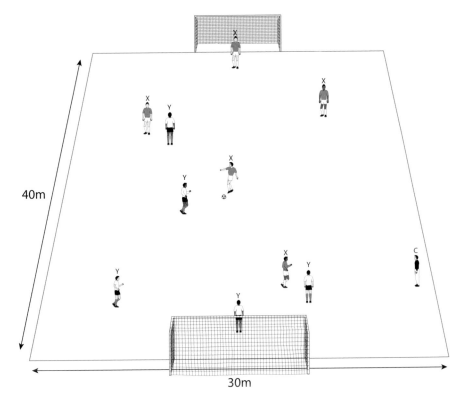

Organisation: Set out a 30 x 40m area. Play 5 v 5 or 6 v 6 inside the area.

Equipment: Bibs, marker cones, football, goals.

Description: Play as a 5 v 5 but points are scored per consecutive pass. 1 pass = 1 point, 2 passes = 2 points and so on. A goal = 5 points, and combination play is encouraged, e.g. 2 passes and a goal = 7 points. The first team to 21 points wins.

Coaching points: Create space to make passing easier. Look to make accurate passes to score extra points. Shoot at goal whenever you have the chance to get maximum points. Apply pressure to the ball when not in possession to limit points scored by the other team.

Progressions: Limit players to two or three touches. Add first-time finish rule.

>>> 46 – 58 – 74 – 99

session 93 ice hockey soccer

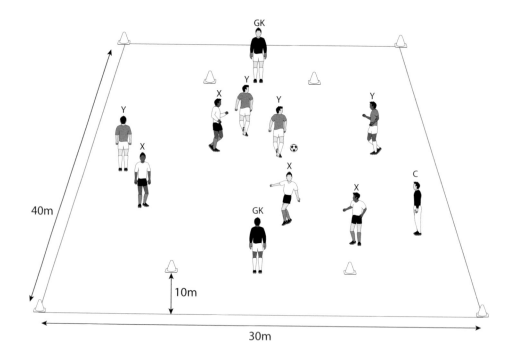

Organisation: Set out a 30 x 40m area. Arrange players into a 4 v 4 with goalkeepers inside the area with the goals at either end moved 10m forward into the playing area so there is space to play behind each goal.

Equipment: Bibs, marker cones, football.

Description: Play 4 v 4, with goalkeepers, with teams attacking either end. Teams may play behind each goal and are able to attempt to score from either the front or the back of the goal.

Coaching points: Play wide and around the goal to create an attack from another angle. Defending team need to have awareness of attacks coming from different areas of the pitch. Be alive to any rebounds or if the ball comes through from behind the goal.

Progressions: Make the goals smaller to make it more difficult to score. Teams must make three consecutive passes before attempting to score. Once a team scores through the front of the goal, they must then attempt to score from behind the goal and alternate sides each time.

>>> 38 – 55 – 76 – 90

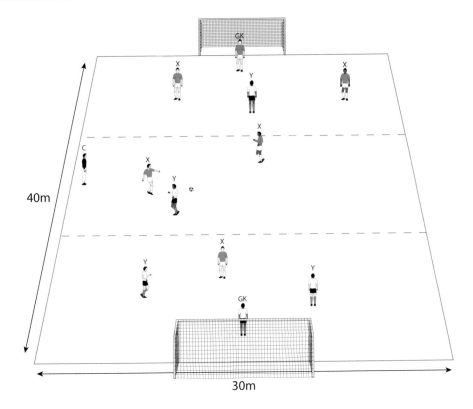

Organisation: Set out a 30 x 40m area and divide it into three sections. Play 5 v 5 plus goalkeepers with two defenders, two midfielders and one striker in the sections set out as shown in the diagram.

Equipment: Bibs, marker cones, football, goals.

Description: Teams play 5 v 5 trying to score in the opponent's goal. Once the ball has entered a different section it cannot be passed back across the line, encouraging forward play. For example, if the ball is played from defence to midfield, it cannot then be passed back into the defensive third.

Coaching points: Encourage positive, attacking play. Players to make space in their section by going wide and deep. Defenders try to close the ball quickly to prevent the forward pass.

Progressions: Allow the player who passes the ball into the next area to follow his pass and play in the next section. Limit players to a first-time finish, encouraging team play.

>>> 48 – 59 – 71 – 74

session 95 all out attack

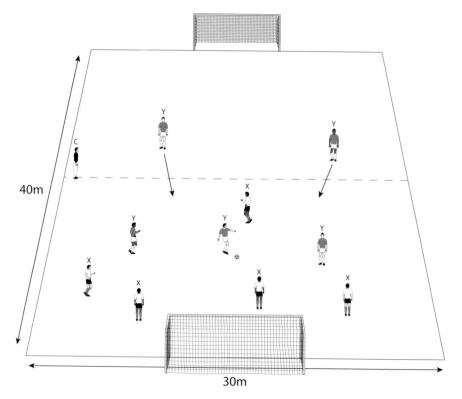

Organisation: Set out a 30 x 40m area, with a halfway line and a small goal at either end. Organise teams into 5 v 5, no goalkeepers.

Equipment: Bibs, marker cones, football, goals.

Description: To score a goal all players from the attacking team must cross the centre line before a shot can be taken. If the defending team wins the ball they can counterattack, but if the ball goes out of play or a goal is scored, the coach then throws a new ball into the empty half of the area.

Coaching points: Get players forward quickly to support the play and try to score. Get defenders behind the ball to protect the goal. Press the ball quickly to force an error and regain possession.

Progressions: Add goalkeepers. Introduce a first-touch finish rule. Limit players to two or three touches.

>>> 51 – 54 – 73 – 94

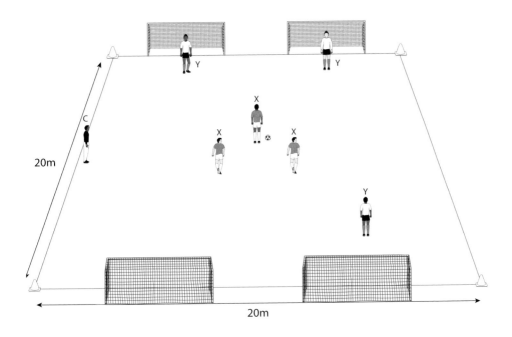

Organisation: Set out a 20 x 20m area, with four small goals placed in the four corners of the area. Teams play 3 v 3 inside the area.

Equipment: Bibs, marker cones, football, goals.

Description: The X players attack and try to score in any of the four goals. The Y players defend but cannot tackle the X players – they are only allowed to move to cover and block the four goals. Play for 5 minutes then change roles; whichever team scores the most goals is the winner.

Coaching points: Play with your head up, so that you can switch the point of attack quickly. Attackers – move the ball quickly to attack the open goal. Defenders – organise and cover the goals as a team.

Progressions: Limit X players to two touches. Allow Y players to tackle and if they win possession the X players become defenders. Introduce a one-touch finish rule.

>>> 23 – 74 – 83 – 84

session 97 cross over

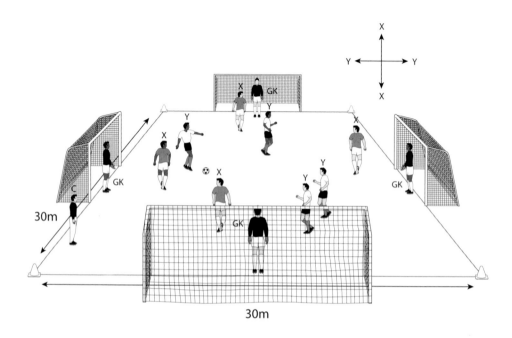

Organisation: Set out a 30 x 30m area with goals on each side of the area.

Equipment: Bibs, marker cones, football, goals.

Description: Play 4 v 4 inside the area with goalkeepers in each goal. X's can only score in the top and bottom goals and Y's can only score in the left and right goals.

Coaching points: Shoot as often as possible. Hit the target. Shoot using laces. Try to defend both goals. Change the point of attack by switching play.

Progressions: Increase difficulty by reducing the size of the goals. Limit players to two or three touches. Add first-time finish rule.

>>> 49 – 50 – 60 – 78

session 98 diagonal passing

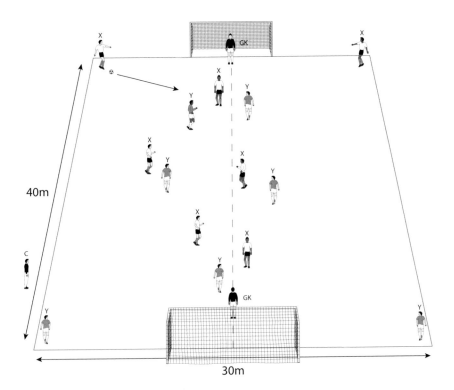

Organisation: Set out a 30 x 40m area with a centre line running from goal to goal, through the middle of the area separating the area into two halves.

Equipment: Bibs, marker cones, football, goals.

Description: The object of the game is to develop diagonal passing in order to encourage players to create space and movement off the ball. The team in possession of the ball must make at least one diagonal pass from one side of the area to the other and across the dividing line of cones before they can attempt to score a goal.

Coaching points: When a player runs across the field, encourage teammates to try to exploit the spaces created. Passes and runs should be diagonal. Players should call for the ball. If the pass is not 'on', the ball carrier should fake to pass and take it himself.

Progressions: Take out the middle line. Limit players to two or three touches. Attackers can score only from a pass from the other side of the field and shoot with a one-touch finish.

>>> 52 – 60 – 74 – 87

session 99 floating wingers

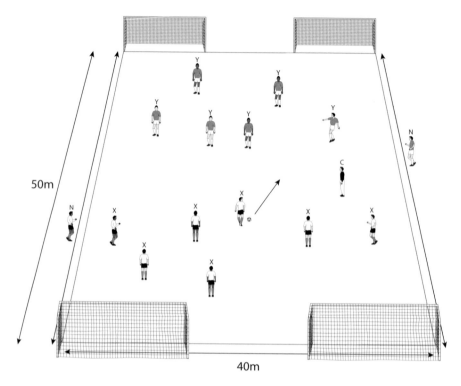

Organisation: Set out a 40 x 50m area with two goals 5m wide at each end of the field as shown in the diagram. Play 7 v 7 in the middle area with two floating players (N) on the outside of the area. The floating players play with the team that has possession.

Equipment: Bibs, marker cones, football, goals.

Description: The object of the game is to score in one of the two opposing goals. This may be achieved by playing within the area or by getting the ball wide to a floating player to cross or shoot on goal.

Coaching points: Switch the ball to the weak side (when attacking). Open up the field by receiving the ball side on (when attacking). Keep possession by spreading out side-to-side and end-to-end (when attacking). Defender/goalkeeper on the weak side acts as cover and support until ball gets there (when defending).

Progressions: When a team has possession, the other team must drop back two of its players to defend the goal. The floating players are restricted to two touches. The team in possession can score only from a cross by a floating player.

>>> 44 – 70 – 100 – 101

the wing game

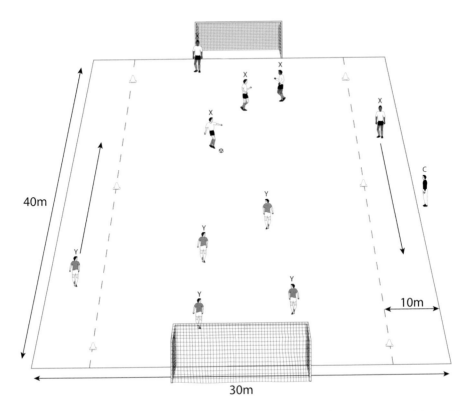

40m

30m

10m

Organisation: Set out a 30 x 40m area with two 10m 'channels' on either side of the central area, as shown in the diagram. Position one player for the X team in one channel, and one player from the Y team in the other.

Equipment: Bibs, marker cones, football, goal.

Description: Teams try to score against the opponent by using the wide zones. Use one player in the channel who must touch the ball at least once before the side can score. Players cannot score from the wing, but must pass the ball back into the field of play for someone else to score.

Coaching points: Passing. Creating space (awareness). Decision making. Communication (teamwork).

Progressions: Have a neutral player in the zone; this player is on both teams. Allow one defender into the channel. Restrict amount of time or distance in the channel.

>>> 49 – 63 – 90 – 101

session 101 wing play

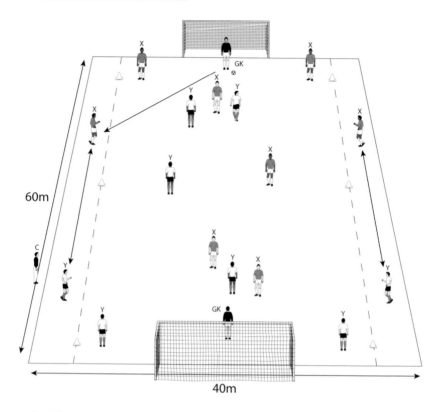

Organisation: Set out a 40 x 60m area with 5m channels along each sideline. Station one player from each team in each channel. Play 7 v 7 in the central area with a goalkeeper at each end.

Equipment: Bibs, marker cones, football, goals.

Description: The aim is to play through your wide player and try to score in the opposing goal. Each team has a player in the wide zones that play 1 v 1 in that area when they receive the ball, acting as a full back when defending and a winger when attacking. Both teams can only score from a cross from the wide player.

Coaching points: Get the ball to the wide player as quickly as possible. Use dribbling skills and moves to beat an opponent when playing 1 v 1 in the channels. Make decoy runs such as the cross-over or diagonal run to lose your defender.

Progressions: Introduce a first-time finish rule. Limit players to two or three touches. Introduce a neutral player who can enter the wide areas to create a 2 v 1 against the full back.

>>> 51 – 72 – 99 – 100

SESSION PLANS

The following list of numbers relate to the sessions in the book and shows which games we feel work well together to make up one session. At the bottom of each page throughout the book we have matched each game with four others in order to create a full session of games and practices, which would last for a minimum of one hour. They are listed again here for you to use as a quick guide.

Passing practices are linked to other passing games and small-sided games which are based around making passes, and subsequently the same applies for the sessions which focus on other techniques like dribbling, turning or shooting.

This is simply a guide, so please feel free to mix and match the sessions to suit what you feel will most benefit your players and help them to get the most out of your sessions.

As previously mentioned, the warm-ups tend to work well with all sessions as they are inclusive games based around movement and mobility.

Practising dribbling and running with the ball will help to enhance a player's confidence when working with the ball at their feet and under pressure during a competitive match.

Fun football games (from page 35)

Session 21: 27 – 30 – 77 – 91
Session 22: 28 – 32 – 68 – 78
Session 23: 35 – 38 – 89 – 96
Session 24: 26 – 37 – 66 – 78
Session 25: 36 – 46 – 81 – 90
Session 26: 24 – 33 – 52 – 80
Session 27: 21 – 40 – 70 – 77
Session 28: 22 – 32 – 62 – 91
Session 29: 23 – 28 – 64 – 83
Session 30: 27 – 39 – 44 – 85
Session 31: 25 – 38 – 63 – 83
Session 32: 22 – 29 – 62 – 84
Session 33: 26 – 77 – 78 – 80
Session 34: 31 – 48 – 81 – 90
Session 35: 23 – 66 – 69 – 98
Session 36: 25 – 35 – 52 – 88
Session 37: 24 – 60 – 69 – 97
Session 38: 31 – 63 – 99 – 100
Session 39: 30 – 40 – 83 – 85
Session 40: 37 – 39 – 76 – 90
Session 41: 44 – 51 – 71 – 79
Session 42: 52 – 79 – 81 – 87
Session 43: 50 – 59 – 74 – 92
Session 44: 41 – 45 – 72 – 94
Session 45: 41 – 42 – 82 – 89
Session 46: 25 – 48 – 87 – 88
Session 47: 26 – 71 – 75 – 93
Session 48: 34 – 49 – 80 – 97
Session 49: 41 – 75 – 82 – 100
Session 50: 37 – 43 – 91 – 97
Session 51: 47 – 73 – 86 – 101
Session 52: 36 – 42 – 59 – 83
Session 53: 55 – 61 – 94 – 95
Session 54: 53 – 57 – 64 – 86
Session 55: 53 – 58 – 65 – 96
Session 56: 54 – 70 – 88 – 92
Session 57: 54 – 60 – 67 – 93
Session 58: 55 – 61 – 69 – 86
Session 59: 43 – 52 – 70 – 96
Session 60: 37 – 57 – 67 – 98
Session 61: 51 – 53 – 58 – 86
Session 62: 32 – 65 – 77 – 80
Session 63: 31 – 38 – 66 – 78
Session 64: 29 – 54 – 68 – 88
Session 65: 28 – 55 – 62 – 91

Session 66: 35 – 63 – 40 – 85
Session 67: 31 – 58 – 60 – 76
Session 68: 22 – 30 – 64 – 96
Session 69: 35 – 58 – 70 – 94
Session 70: 27 – 59 – 95 – 99

Small-sided football games (from page 91)

Session 71: 41 – 47 – 72 – 87
Session 72: 44 – 49 – 74 – 101
Session 73: 47 – 51 – 82 – 92
Session 74: 43 – 50 – 72 – 98
Session 75: 47 – 82 – 87 – 99
Session 76: 40 – 50 – 79 – 93
Session 77: 21 – 62 – 68 – 80
Session 78: 24 – 33 – 60 – 77
Session 79: 42 – 45 – 76 – 101
Session 80: 26 – 66 – 77 – 85
Session 81: 25 – 42 – 45 – 89
Session 82 49 – 74 – 75 – 97
Session 83: 39 – 64 – 65 – 84
Session 84: 29 – 36 – 63 – 83
Session 85: 30 – 33 – 77 – 80
Session 86: 54 – 56 – 61 – 95
Session 87: 44 – 46 – 75 – 82
Session 88: 39 – 62 – 70 – 96
Session 89: 22 – 43 – 79 – 81
Session 90: 25 – 34 – 82 – 100
Session 91: 28 – 55 – 64 – 83
Session 92: 46 – 58 – 74 – 99
Session 93: 38 – 55 – 76 – 90
Session 94: 48 – 59 – 71 – 74
Session 95: 51 – 54 – 73 – 94
Session 96: 23 – 74 – 83 – 84
Session 97: 49 – 50 – 60 – 78
Session 98: 52 – 60 – 74 – 87
Session 99: 44 – 70 – 100 – 101
Session 100: 49 – 63 – 90 – 101
Session 101: 51 – 72 – 99 – 100